Attuned Lea

Rabbinic Texts on Habits of the Heart in Learning Interactions

Jᴇᴡɪsʜ Iᴅᴇɴᴛɪᴛʏ ɪɴ Pᴏsᴛ-Mᴏᴅᴇʀɴ Sᴏᴄɪᴇᴛʏ

ACADEMIC
STUDIES
PRESS

Attuned Learning

Rabbinic Texts on Habits of the Heart in Learning Interactions

Elie HOLZER

BOSTON / 2017

Library of Congress Cataloging-in-Publication Data:
A bibliographic record for this title is available
from the Library of Congress.

ISBN 978-1-61811-480-8 (cloth)
ISBN 978-1-61811-635-2 (paper)
ISBN 978-1-61811-481-5 (electronic)

Cover design by Ivan Grave

Published by Academic Studies Press in 2016, paperback 2017
 28 Montfern Avenue
Brighton, MA 02135, USA
press@academicstudiespress.com
www.academicstudiespress.com

To Suzi, Lital, Vered, Avigail, and Noam
For being the bliss of my earthly existence

There is an initiative trust, an investment of belief, underwritten by previous experience but epistemologically exposed and psychologically hazardous, in the meaningfulness, in the "seriousness" of the facing or, strictly speaking, adverse text. We venture a leap: we grant *ab initio* that there is "something there" to be understood [...] All understanding [. . .] starts with an act of trust. This confiding will, ordinarily, be instantaneous and unexamined, but it has a complex base. It is an operative convention which derives from a sequence of phenomenological assumptions about the coherence of the world, about the presence of meaning in very different, perhaps formally antithetical semantic systems, about the validity of analogy and parallel.

—George Steiner, *After Babel:*
Aspects of Language and Translation, 312

To quote is to reflect on what has been said before, and unless we do that, we speak in a vacuum where no human voice can make a sound.

—Alberto Manguel,
The Library at Night, 224

The search for references to universality in the Scriptures and in the texts of the spoken Law still derives from the process of assimilation. These texts, across two thousand years of commentary, still have something other to say.

—Emmanuel Levinas,
Assimilation and New Culture, 287

Table of Contents

ATTUNED ACKNOWLEDGMENTS

There are two types of memories. One is sterile: it feels like a fixation of the past; it is a memory wherein the past dominates the present and paralyzes it. And there is a second type of memory: a vivid memory, one that is at work in the present; a memory that affects the present and nourishes it, and by which the present, in some sense, governs the past.

The completion of a book is a time of reminiscence.

A time of *hakarat hatov*, of gratitude toward all those who, through past and present encounters, have nourished this book.

Our encounters took place throughout several decades.

They have amassed as a slow-growing awareness.

During classes.

In *chavruta* learning.

I was a student.

I served as the teacher.

I studied as a *chavruta* partner.

Precious moments of learning.

Touched by something ineffable.

Moments of learning with and from friends, teachers, students, and texts.

Marcel Proust writes that some of our childhood reading experiences leave behind in us vivid images of those places and times. Similarly, some learning moments live inside me as fragments and images.

Of faces, of spaces, of times, and of emotions.

They are living glimpses of the past that enlighten my teaching, my learning, and my research.

These memories are *lived* time.

Kairos overcomes Chronos, to reconnect with the voice and the face of the beloved teacher, with the insights offered by texts, with the smiling faces of learning partners, and with moments of excitement in the wake of students' comments.

Chapters Three and Four discuss paired learning. They are dedicated to my friend and *chavruta* partner, Gabriel Strenger. Your ways of being and of doing in our years of *chavruta* learning have nurtured my sensitivity toward spiritual and ethical dimensions of *chavruta* learning.

Chapter Five, which discusses the idea of transformative teaching, is dedicated to my friend and colleague Gail Dorph. Your wisdom of practice and your passion for people's learning were critical in helping me think and re-conceptualize the study of rabbinic texts for teachers' professional growth.

Chapter Six discusses students' awareness and is dedicated to the many students I have been privileged to interact with, since my very first hesitative steps as a teacher. Many fragments of our learning interactions continue to dwell inside me as a conscious and unconscious silent presence thanks to your curiosity, your questions, and your contributions to our shared explorations.

Chapter Seven attends to the mysterious impact of the face. This chapter is devoted with feelings of longing to my beloved teacher, Rav Moshe Botschko, of blessed memory. Since his passing away, his face has become an increasingly living presence. A glimpse of that radiant face implanted in me the seeds of three most precious gifts:

A trust in the texts of our tradition: that many of these texts have something to say that deeply matters for life, sometimes beyond what first meets the eye.

A trust in myself as a learner of that tradition; in my moral-religious obligation to make the text speak through the filter of human reason and ethical sensitivity.

A trust in my ability to innovate and to generate new meanings.

In the process of crystalizing disparate thoughts into a cohesive book, I have been fortunate to benefit from the friendship of Professor Marc Brettler and Professor Avi Sagi. Each of them spared no effort to assist and provide me with wise advice whenever it was needed. Each taught me new meanings of attuned colleagueship.

Last but certainly not least: Sari Steinberg joined this project as editor. Her talent competes only with her gentleness, and her ability to hear the voice of spoken and written words is a true model of human attunement.

Jerusalem, Adar/March 2015

Part One

CONCEPTUAL FRAMEWORKS

Chapter One

THE CONCEPT OF ATTUNED LEARNING[1]

> The main thing about schools is that they are one of the very few remaining public interactional spaces in which people are still engaged with each other in the reciprocal, though organizationally patterned, labor of producing meaning—indeed, the core meaning of self-identity.[2]
>
> —*Philip Wexler*

> Instead of teaching, I told stories. Anything to keep them quiet and in their seats. They thought I was teaching. I thought I was teaching. I was learning.[3]
>
> —*Frank McCourt*

You—the reader of this book—are familiar with the whispering voice of your consciousness. Despite its evasiveness, you allow it to lead you in your social relationships. What would happen if you paid close attention to that whisper as you moved through your daily interactions, especially in educational settings—whether as a teacher, a student, or a co-learner? The concept of *attuned learning* conveys this type of deliberate alertness to an individual's own mental, emotional, and physical workings, and awareness of others within the complexities of learning interactions.[4] This

---

[1] In most cases of unspecified gender, this book favors the feminine pronoun, in an effort to balance the masculine-dominated language of ancient texts and scholars.

[2] Philip Wexler, *Becoming Somebody: Toward a Social Psychology of School* (London and Washington DC: Falmer, 1992), 10.

[3] Frank McCourt, *Teacher Man: A Memoir* (Old Tappan: Scribner, 2006), 19.

[4] The term "attuned learning" is inspired by the title Michael Fishbane, *Sacred*

term has been used in recent years regarding attention *by* teachers *to* students' different learning styles and capacities; but it can be expanded and enriched so that it becomes an essential human disposition, the humane dimensions of learning interactions, not only for teachers but also for students and co-learners. This type of deliberate self-cultivation that infuses teaching and learning with ethical and spiritual dimensions is a new discovery — yet it reflects values that were embraced in ancient times. This book looks from a contemporary perspective at rabbinic texts that seem, by design, to prescribe attuned learning as a way of raising individuals' introspection and their attitudes toward each other within the actual learning dynamic. These dispositions, then, also become part of the individuals' lives beyond the classroom or the *beit midrash*.[5]*

This book, like the author's practice-oriented philosophy of Jewish learning, focuses on the potential cultivation of learners' ethical dispositions* in and through their interactions with texts, teachers, and co-learners.[6] The integration of the pedagogical with the ethical, and imaginative and critical thinking with human interactions, forges a philosophy that fosters habits of the mind, the hand, and the heart, and assumes that learning through inner as well as outer dialogue is a worthy way of living. All of this has led to the conceptualization and design of a model of *chavruta** learning (the study of texts by a pair of learners) comprised of three categories of practices that can be taught and learned: intrapersonal (an individual's perceptions, feelings, and ethical sensibility),

---

Attunement: A Jewish Theology (Chicago and London: University of Chicago Press, 2008).

[5]   Terms annotated with a star (*) are elaborated in the "Glossary of Technical and Foreign Terms and Language Usage."

[6]   Elie Holzer, "Ethical dispositions in Text Study," *Journal of Moral Education* 36, no. 1 (2007): 37–49; Elie Holzer, "What Connects 'Good' Teaching, Text Study and Hevruta Learning? A Conceptual Argument," *Journal of Jewish Education* 72 (2006): 1–22; Elie Holzer, "Allowing the Text to do its Pedagogical Work: Connecting Moral Education and Interpretive Activity," *Journal of Moral Education* 6, no. 4 (2007): 497–514; Elie Holzer, "Educational aspects of hermeneutical activity in text study," *Modes of Educational Translation*, in *Studies in Jewish Education*, ed. Jonathan Cohen and Elie Holzer (Jerusalem: Magnes Press, 2008–2009), 205–240.

interpersonal (interactions with others such as a teacher, student, and/or co-learner), and textual-interpretive (engagement with the subject matter), as well as the discussion of the formative ethical aspects of these practices.[7]

Rabbinic literature illuminates this book's exploration of another essential component of this philosophy. While other scholars have examined some aspects of learning and of ethics in rabbinic culture, this book uniquely interprets rabbinic texts that concern habits of the heart—the marriage of interdependence, emotion, and self-awareness in individuals' attitudes toward each other and toward the subject matter within the actual learning dynamic.

Contextual Awareness and Ethical Sensitivity

Philosopher Martha Nussbaum discusses moral attentiveness as central to living a good life. According to Nussbaum, "perception without responsibility is dangerously free-floating, even as duty without perception is blunt and blind."[8] Ethical engagement implies awareness of a given situation, not only to achieve the correct action, but as a valuable aptitude in its own right.[9] Similarly, attuned

---

[7] Holzer, "Ethical dispositions in Text Study"; Miriam Raider-Roth and Elie Holzer, "Learning to be Present: How Hevruta Learning Can Activate Teachers' Relationships to Self, Other and Text," *The Journal of Jewish Education* 75, no. 3 (2009): 216–239; Elie Holzer with Orit Kent, *A Philosophy of Havruta: Understanding and Teaching the Art of Text Study in Pairs* (Brighton: Academic Studies Press, 2013); Elie Holzer, "Welcoming Opposition: *Havruta* Learning and Montaigne's *The Art of Discussion*," *The Journal of Moral Education* 44, no. 1 (2015): 64–80.

[8] Martha C. Nussbaum, *Love's Knowledge: Essays on Philosophy and Literature* (New York: Oxford University Press 1990), 155.

[9] This view is grounded in Aristotelian ethics, particularly in Aristotle's concept of *phronesis*. According to Aristotle, a virtuous person is someone who consciously chooses the virtuous action. This view of ethics emphasizes the moral character of the person, in contrast to deontological views of ethics, which emphasize duties or rules, and in contrast to consequentialist views of ethics, which emphasize the consequences of actions. Aristotle's moral philosophy is therefore intertwined with his view of moral habits or dispositions. According to Aristotle, these dispositions cannot be taught and do not exist innately in humans. They can be nurtured and become stable

learning involves an ability to discern and to act keenly in the intrapersonal, interpersonal, and textual-interpretive realms within particular learning situations.[10] Attuned learning thereby connects to a number of educational, psychological, and philosophical theories regarding reflection and ethical dimensions of learning interactions.

Theoretical Underpinnings: Reflection as a Form of Mindfulness

For over three decades, reflection has been a topic of constant research and practical implementation in teachers' professional development. The works of theorists such as John Dewey, Donald Schon, and Paulo Freire—to cite just three examples—have been instrumental in redefining teaching as a reflective practice and in conceptualizing reflection as a form of self-awareness that lies at the heart of what it means to understand the practice of teaching.[11]

---

traits of an individual's character through habituation of ongoing moral behavior. For a philosophical discussion of phronesis in relation to teaching, see Joseph Dunne, *Back to the Rough Ground: Practical Judgment and the Lure of Technique* (Notre Dame: University of Notre Dame Press, 2001). For the similarities between this view and ethical theories in rabbinic literature, and for its implications in the context of text study and *chavruta* learning, see Holzer, "Ethical Aspects of Text Study"; Elie Holzer, "'Either a Hevruta Partner of Death'—A Critical View on the Interpersonal Dimensions of Hevruta Learning," *The Journal of Jewish Education* 75, no. 2 (2009): 130–149.

[10] For the co-creation of relationships and learning, and the discernment of the interpersonal and the subject matter as keys to learning, see James G. Greeno and Melissa S. Gresalfi, "Opportunities to Learn in Practice and Identity," in *Assessment, Equity, and Opportunity to Learn*, ed. Pamela A. Moss, Diana C. Pullin, Edward H. Haertel, James Paul Gee, and Lauren Jones Young (New York: Cambridge University Press, 2008), 171: "The ways that individuals are positioned with respect to others and the content of the activity is inseparable from their engagement with the content itself. Thus, learning involves participation with both interpersonal and informational aspects of an activity." For a related genre see Michael DePaul, "Argument and Perception: The Role of Literature in Moral Inquiry," *Journal of Philosophy* 85 (1988): 552–565.

[11] Nona Lyons, ed., *Handbook of Reflection and Reflective Inquiry Mapping a Way of Knowing for Professional Reflective Inquiry* (New York: Springer, 2010).

Drawing on Aristotle's concept of *phronesis*, educational researchers Fred Korthagen and Jos Kessels discuss the nature of perceptual knowledge, which requires discrimination and judgment but also flexibility and congruency to the situation at hand.[12] Such knowledge is acquired through experience and develops into an individual's self-perceived ability for insight in real-life situations.[13] A generative example of awareness by a teacher in the midst of teaching and learning interactions is discussed by educational philosopher David Hawkins, who conceptualizes the roles of the teacher (*I*), the student (*Thou*), and the subject matter (*It*) in their reciprocal interactions.[14] Hawkins uses this triangular representation as a heuristic framework to help teachers grow into "diagnosticians of learning" by refining their perception and heightening their awareness of students' learning and the complex intertwinement of the three elements.[15] While the interactions have reciprocal effects, teachers have the greatest impact on the dynamic. The teacher brings the *It* into the room, facilitates the learner's relationship with the subject matter, prompts, questions and offers feedback to help the learner progress through it. For Hawkins, being attuned to these interactions allows a teacher to be intellectually and psychologically available to himself, the students, and the subject matter. Hawkins shows that the teacher's awareness of and concern for the student emanates from his caring about the student's learning of the subject

---

[12]   Jos P. A. M. Kessels and Fred A. J. Korthagen, "The Relationship between Theory and Practice: Equality or Inequality?," in *Teacher Education for Equality*, ed. Edvard Befring (Oslo: Oslo College, 1996), 357–365; Jos P. A. M. Kessels and Fred A. J. Korthagen, "The Relationship between Theory and Practice: Back to the Classics," *Educational Researcher* 25, no. 3 (1996): 17–22.

[13]   Philosopher Martha Nussbaum describes a person who possesses perceptual knowledge as someone who "inhabits the human world" (Martha C. Nussbaum, *The Fragility of Goodness: Luck and Ethics in Greek Tragedy and Philosophy* [Cambridge: Cambridge University Press, 1986], 314). See also Gary D. Fenstermacher, "The Knower and the Known: The Nature of Knowledge in Research on Teaching," in *Review of Research in Education* 20, ed. Linda Darling-Hammond (Washington, DC: AERA, 1994), 3–56.

[14]   David Hawkins, "I, Thou and It," in *The Informed Vision: Essays on Learning and Human Nature*, ed. David Hawkins (New York: Agathon Press, 1974), 48–62.

[15]   Ibid., 55.

matter. Thus the relationship between teacher and student is imbued with confidence, trust, and respect.[16] These qualities do not exist prior to, but rather emerge from, their teaching and learning interactions.

Educational researchers Fred Korthagen and Angelo Vasalos discuss the limitations of analytic models of reflection, which provide teachers with a better understanding of their practice, but which do not significantly contribute to their professional efficacy. Korthagen and Vasalos attribute this shortcoming to the emphasis on abstract concepts at the cost of teachers' ability to establish connections within concrete classroom situations. Thus, a teacher could understand the concept of *caring* and its importance for her relationship with students, and still fail to develop such relationships.[17] The researchers suggest that teachers develop and nurture the inner strata of their personalities and their professional identities, which will have a positive impact on their interactions in real classroom life.[18]

Particularly relevant to attuned learning is the concept of *presence*, which educational psychologists Carol Rodgers and Miriam Raider-Roth define as the teacher's "experience of bringing one's whole self to full attention so as to perceive what is happening in the moment."[19] Grounded and reflected in several philosophical

---

[16] Ibid., 56.

[17] Fred A. J. Korthagen and Angelo Vasalos, "From Reflection to Presence and Mindfulness: Thirty Years of Developments Concerning the Concept of Reflection in Teacher Education," (paper presented at the EARLI Conference, Amsterdam, August 2009), available at http://www.kernreflectie.nl/Media/pdf/EARLI%20paper.pdf.

[18] Paulien C. Meijer, Fred A. J. Korthagen, and Angelo Vasalos, "Supporting Presence in Teacher Education: The Connection between the Personal and Professional Aspects of Teaching," *Teaching and Teacher Education* 25, no. 2 (2009): 297–308. Other scholars have become aware of the role feelings, instead of only "thinking about the feelings." See Antonio Damasio, *The Feeling of What Happens: Body and Emotion in the Making of Consciousness* (London: Heinemann, 1999), 279–295.

[19] Carol R. Rodgers and Miriam B. Raider-Roth, "Presence in Teaching," *Teachers and Teaching: Theory and Practice* 12, no. 3 (2006): 267. See also "Human consciousness [. . .] is always situated; and the situated person inevitably

and spiritual traditions, the essence of this idea is the ability to be present simultaneously to oneself and to the environment; it is a state of being in which an individual is "sensitive to the flow of events."[20] In that regard, attuned learning is a form of mindfulness.[21]

Theoretical Underpinnings: Ethical Aspects of Learning Interactions

Nel Noddings and other educational philosophers have challenged and criticized the discourse of technical rationality in education—a view of teaching as a professional activity consisting

---

engages with others, reaches out and grasps the phenomena surrounding him/her from a particular vantage point and against a particular background consciousness" (Maxine Green, *The Dialectic of Freedom* [New York: Teachers College Press, 1988], 21). Green writes about "wide-awakeness" with regard to the professional preparation of teachers: "If teachers today are to initiate young people into an ethical existence, they themselves must attend more fully than they normally have to their own lives and its requirements; they have to break with the mechanical life, to overcome their own submergence in the habitual" (Maxine Green, *Teacher as Stranger: Educational Philosophy for the Modern Age* [Belmont: Wadsworth Publishing Company, 1973], 46). Alfred Schutz uses the term "wide-awakeness" to denote the consciousness that originates in full attention to life and its requirements (Alfred Schutz, *On Phenomenology and Social Relations*, ed. Helmut R. Wagner [Chicago: University of Chicago Press, 1970], 69; Alfred Schutz, *Collected Papers Vol. I*, ed. Maurice Natanson [The Hague: Martinus Nijhoff, 1967], 213).

20 Rodgers and Raider-Roth, "Presence in Teaching," 235. See also A-Hameed Almaas, *Essence: The Diamond Approach to Inner Realization* (York Beach: Samuel Weiser, 1986); A-Hameed Almaas, *The Unfolding Now: Realizing Your True Nature through the Practice of Presence* (Boston and London: Shambala, 2008); Peter Senge, C. Otto Scharmer, Joseph Jaworski and Betty Sue Flowers, *Presence: Exploring Profound Change in People, Organizations and Society* (London: Nicolas Brealey, 2004).

21 Mindfulness differs from a more detached conceptual awareness in that its mode of functioning is more perceptual or pre-reflective. See Kirk Warren Brown and Richard M. Ryan, "The Benefit of Being Present: Mindfulness and Its Role in Psychological Well-being," *Journal of Personality and Social Psychology* 84 (2003): 822–848; Christopher K. Germer, Ronald D. Siegel, and Paul R. Fulton, eds., *Mindfulness and Psychotherapy* (New York: Guilford Press, 2005).

of instrumental problem-solving by the application of scientific theory and technique—for its lack of caring, compassion, and passion.[22] Social critics and philosophers such as Ira Shor and Paulo Freire, and educational thinkers including Harvey Svi Shapiro, lament the loss of the teacher-student relationship as a priority in educational discourse.[23] Social and feminist activist bell hooks calls for a reconsideration of teaching practice, asking whether there is room for spirituality in teaching and in education.[24] Concern for one another comprises the ethical aspects of the teaching and learning interactions.[25] These voices are but a sample of those expressing concern about the increasingly technical discourse of education in general and of teaching in particular. Instrumental models of education are perceived to originate in values and concepts from consumerism and market economy, which frame the educational experience as a business transaction, with the goods (information) going *from* an educational supplier (teacher) *to* a client (student).[26]

---

[22]   Nel Noddings, *Caring: A Feminine Approach to Ethics and Moral Education* (Berkeley: University of California Press, 1987). Noddings is only one among other similar voices. See, for example, Kenneth M. Zeichner, *Educating Teachers for Cultural Diversity* (Michigan State University: National Center for Research, 1993).

[23]   Ira Shor, *Empowering Education* (Chicago: University of Chicago Press, 1992); Paolo Freire, *Pedagogy of the Oppressed* (New York: Continuum, 1993); Harvey Svi Shapiro, *Losing Heart The Moral and Spiritual Miseducation of America's Children* (London: Routledge, 2004).

[24]   bell hooks, *Teaching Community: A Pedagogy of Hope* (London: Routledge, 2003).

[25]   This work uses the concepts of dispositions (Footnote 9). However my use of "ethics" in reference to a person's attunement toward others is inspired by the philosophy of Emmanuel Levinas, according to whom ethics lies in this fundamental openness to what lies beyond oneself: "It is the meaning of the beyond, of transcendence, and not of ethics that our study seeks. It finds this meaning in ethics" (Emmanuel Levinas, *Of God Who Comes To Mind* [Stanford: Stanford University Press, 1998], 200). The intertwinement between the ethical and transcendence is addressed in Chapter Four, Footnote 26, and Chapter Eight, Footnote 12.

[26]   Jane Tompkins, "Learning from the Workplace: Professional Life as an Opportunity for Personal Growth," in *Living the Questions: Essays Inspired by*

And yet, discussion of relational and dialogical aspects of education is not a new frontier. Earlier works have already portrayed the educational experience as having subjective, contextual, and holistic qualities. They also have demonstrated that learning establishes and is nurtured by relationships, whether among a teacher and students or between two learners.[27] This book seeks to contribute to this school of thought by hearkening back to ancient times and connecting it to time-honored themes as well as to contemporary perspectives on educational discourse and practices. Through this book, less experienced teachers and students may become more aware of learning interactions, and experienced educators and co-learners may want to think further about some of their experiences. This book is unapologetically passionate about ethical and spiritual concerns in teaching and learning, as well as a commitment to seeing attuned learning flourish in the contemporary classroom. It is written for the motivated reader and/or educator for whom education remains an existential passion, who feels enhanced when examining, expanding, or revisiting her own educational beliefs and practices. To that end, it also offers critical reflections to assist in furthering such processes in the wake of its reading.

---

the Life and Work of Parker J. Palmer, ed. Sam M. Intrator (San Francisco: Jossey-Bass, 2005), 89–97. See also the discussion in Chapter Eight, in the section *Teachers' Attuned Teaching*.

[27] Martin Buber, *Between Man and Man* (London: Routledge, 2002); Elaine Riley-Taylor, *Ecology, Spirituality, and Education: Curriculum for Relational Knowing* (New York: Peter Lang, 2002); Andy Hargreaves, "Emotional Geographies of Teaching," *Teachers College Record 103* (2001): 1056–1080. For a discussion of relational theories of teaching, see Raider-Roth and Holzer, "Learning to be Present." Another source for understanding the intersubjective nature of instruction is the philosophical hermeneutics of Hans-Georg Gadamer, *Truth and Method* (New York: Continuum, 1996). For its application in Jewish education, see Deborah Kerdeman, "Some Thoughts about Hermeneutics and Jewish Religious Education," *Religious Education* 93, no. 1 (1998): 29–43; Jon A. Levisohn, "Openness and Commitment: Hans-Georg Gadamer and the Teaching of Jewish Texts," *Journal of Jewish Education* 67, no. 1–2 (2001): 20–35; and in the context of *chavruta* text study, see Holzer with Kent, *A Philosophy of Havruta*.

How This Book Is Organized

Chapter Two discusses how ancient texts force readers into a new critical awareness of their own attitudes, per the interpretive and literary theories of Hans-Georg Gadamer and Paul Ricoeur. From the vantage point of a contemporary educational researcher, rabbinic texts can be a powerful resource for reawakening aspects of teaching, and modern scholarship of rabbinics provides essential tools in the examination of these texts. The chapter discusses the origins of the work presented in this book, and the methodological tools that have been used in accomplishing its task.

The following chapters provide a literary analysis of late-antiquity rabbinic texts, with original analyses that reveal intra- and interpersonal dimensions of learning interactions for co-learners (Part Two) and for teachers and students (Part Three), and together unfold into an expanded conceptualization of attuned learning.

The Introduction to Part Two integrates the exploration of rabbinic texts that address attuned learning into the broader concepts of collaborative and argumentative learning in Talmudic* and post-Talmudic texts. Chapter Three discusses self-refinement in argumentative learning, through an analysis of rabbinic texts that invite co-learners to reveal their personalities and defend their strongly held opinions while engaging in such learning. At the same time, these texts raise study partners' awareness regarding potential negative effects of this style of learning, such as animosity, hubris, or the clash of egos, and alert them to the necessity of introspection and the cultivation of a complex set of abilities and refined consciousness. Chapter Four analyzes a Talmudic legend that has served for centuries as an icon of co-learning in rabbinic literature. This new reading reveals that it raises critical awareness of co-learners' own expectations of collaborative learning and reveals pitfalls of radically self-serving and controlling attitudes. It sensitizes them to a sincere concern for the joint project of sense-making and a deep investment in the co-learner's learning progress.

The Introduction to Part Three connects attuned learning in teacher-student interactions with rabbinic texts that show a concern for the concrete, subjective, dynamic, and unpredictable—in short, the *experiential*—aspects of teaching and learning. Chapter Five explores the teacher's awareness of transformations that ideally occur within the student, the subject matter, and the teacher through their interactions. Chapter Six discusses disruptions that students may experience in their interactions with teachers and with subject matter, and a student's and the larger community's responsibility for the repair of those disrupted relationships. Chapter Seven focuses on the role played by the visage in the interactions of teacher, student, and subject matter, and the potential to attune teachers and learners to a type of seeing and being-seen. This includes sensitizing them to the personal qualities and the uniqueness of each other and of the subject matter, and helping teachers notice their own projections on, and impressions of, differences in students' facial radiance. Chapter Eight concludes by circling back to discuss the educational significance of attuned learning. Attuned learning demands the cultivation of habits of the heart and of action, as well as patience with the unpredictable nature of human beings' reactions. It can occur only through everyday dilemmas and opportunities offered by learning interactions, by which teachers, students, and co-learners grow in the practice of teaching, of learning, and ultimately of living. The chapter concludes with critical reflections designed to fuel readers' own explorations of ideas elicited by the rabbinic texts, in contemporary educational and cultural contexts.

Chapter Two

READING RABBINIC TEXTS FOR EDUCATION

> The illusion is not in looking for a point of departure but looking for it without presuppositions. There is no philosophy without presuppositions.[1]
> —*Paul Ricoeur*

> Understanding is to be thought less as a subjective act than as participating in an event of tradition, a process of transmission in which past and present are constantly mediated.[2]
> —*Hans-Georg Gadamer*

> Words are effective not because of what they carry in them, but for their latent potential to unlock the accumulated experience of the reader. Words "contain" meanings, but, more important, words potentiate meaning.[3]
> —*Fred Mendelsund*

"What is reading?" asks Louis Althusser in his commentary on *Das Kapital*. This may appear to be a simple question, but Althusser warns us: "As there is no such thing as an innocent reading, we must say what reading we are guilty of."[4] Likewise, Hans-Georg Gadamer, a philosopher of reading and interpretation, insists that in any research project, our first aim should be to articulate an

---

[1]   Paul Ricoeur, *The Symbolism of Evil* (Boston: Beacon Press, 1967), 348.

[2]   Gadamer, *Truth and Method*, 290.

[3]   Fred Mendelsund, *What We See When We Read* (New York: Vintage Books, 2014), 302.

[4]   Louis Althusser and Étienne Balibar, *Reading Capital* (London: NLB, 1970), 14.

awareness of our motives and of our interpretive approach. But, unlike Althusser, Gadamer recognizes that "to imagine that one might ever attain full illumination as to his motives or his interests in questions is to imagine something impossible." Notwithstanding, Gadamer adds:

> In spite of this, it remains a legitimate task to clarify what lies at the basis of our interests as far as possible. Only then are we in a position to understand the statements with which we are concerned [i.e., in the text], precisely insofar as we recognize our own questions in them.[5]

Philosophical Hermeneutics and Reading Ancient Texts

Broadly speaking, philosophical hermeneutics sees history as a living dialogue among past, present, and future, in which texts play a central role, and seeks to ease this infinite communication. It thereby contributes to a distinct form of Jewish educational thinking and to Jewish learning conceptualized as an enactment of such a living dialogue.[6]

While originating as an attempt to theorize the interpretation of texts, philosophical hermeneutics opens a broader scope, offering an epistemology grounded in an interpretive view of both understanding and the self.[7] It raises literary questions regarding

---

[5]   Hans-Georg Gadamer, *Reason in an Age of Science* (Cambridge, MA: MIT Press, 1981), 107–108.

[6]   Holzer with Kent, *A Philosophy of Havruta*, 184–207.

[7]   My work is based on an eclectic synthesis of key concepts of philosophical hermeneutics, especially those found in the works of Hans-Georg Gadamer (1900–2002) and Paul Ricoeur (1913–2005). It is supplemented by more recent literary and philosophical theories on the nature of reading and textual interpretation. See, for example, Terry Eagleton, *After Theory* (New York: Basic Books, 2003). Gadamer and Ricoeur address how interpretation is possible after the metaphysical shift away from the author and after the epistemological shift away from objectivity. For more on the connections between philosophical hermeneutics and literary theory, see Joel Weinsheimer, *Philosophical Hermeneutics and Literary Theory* (New Haven: Yale University Press, 1991); Mario J. Valdes, *Phenomenological Hermeneutics and the Study of Literature* (Toronto: University of Toronto Press, 1987); and Denis Donoghue, *The Practice of Reading* (New Haven: Yale University Press, 1998). Over the

how vested interests of class, gender, or prior belief may influence how we read. It involves questions about types of texts and processes of reading: What is the meaning of a literary text? How relevant to this meaning is the author's intention? Is it possible to understand texts that are culturally and historically alien to us? Is "objective" understanding attainable, or is all understanding relative to the reader's surroundings?

Philosophical hermeneutics also provides important insights about elements of character education in the study of texts.[8]

Does the text shape interpretation, or does interpretation shape the text? Philosophical hermeneutics rejects this either/or approach, instead viewing meaning as the result of a two-way encounter between text and reader. This idea is conveyed by the term *the hermeneutical circle*, in which both reader and text participate. The reader's often-unconscious cultural context, prior history, and everyday experience—what Martin Heidegger calls *fore-knowledge*[9] and Hans-Georg Gadamer calls *fore-meaning* or *preconceptions*— always play a role.[10] Far from being a detached observer, the reader inhabits a sphere that limits and conditions what can be known.

last decades, the field of Jewish education has seen a rise in scholarship building on some of these theories: Levisohn, "Openness and Commitment"; Kerdeman, "Some Thoughts about Hermeneutics and Jewish Religious Education"; Holzer, "Ethical Aspects of Text Study"; and Holzer with Kent, *A Philosophy of Havruta.*

8 See for example the role *bildung* by Hans-Georg Gadamer, *Truth and Method,* which captures the centrality of learning and education as existential categories at the heart of philosophical hermeneutics. For a related discussion on *chavruta* text study, see the section "Havruta Text Study and Formative Practices," in Holzer with Kent, *A Philosophy of Havruta,* 193–207. A seminal work that discusses learning and education from within philosophical hermeneutics is Shaun Gallagher, *Hermeneutics and Education* (Albany: State University of New York Press, 1992).

9 Martin Heidegger, *Being and Time* (New York: Harper Perennial, 1962).

10 Gadamer, *Truth and Method.* It should be emphasized that "preconceptions" are a fundamental constitution of human beings: "Long before we understand ourselves through the process of self-examination, we understand ourselves in a self-evident way in the family, society and state in which we live. The focus of subjectivity is a distorting mirror. The self-awareness of the individual is only a flickering in the closed circuits of historical life. That is why the prejudices

Gadamer's use of the word *horizon* captures the dynamic between the reader and the text in the interpretive process.[11] This term refers to the cultural, linguistic, biographical, and philosophical worlds in which the reader operates, which are limits beyond which she cannot see. It is connected to an individual's established outlook. Texts also have a horizon, as they also reflect the preconceptions of their historical situations.[12] On the basis of this theory, it is possible to move away from a narrow and restricted search for authorial intention, instead exploring the *world* of the text.

Paul Ricoeur distinguishes between the text's *work* and the text's *world*. *Work* refers to something that is crafted in terms of form, genre, and style and that invites methodological examination. In the analysis of a text, the interpreter will look for recurring words and phrases, narrative themes, and theme variations. Ricoeur is interested in particular words that have metaphorical value, which point to meanings hidden below the surface of the writing. Yet, none of these structural elements is meaningful in and of itself; they must be put together to form a meaningful pattern in order to reach full understanding.[13] What a text refers to—its sense—is the *world* of the text. This world is the text's point of reference; it is a perspective,

---

of the individual, far more than his judgments, constitute the historical reality of this being" (Gadamer, *Truth and Method*, 278).

11   Gadamer defines "horizon" as "the range of vision that includes everything that can be seen from a particular vantage point" (Gadamer, *Truth and Method*, 302).

12   Interpreting a text implies a reciprocal movement that takes place between the interpreter's horizon and the horizon she encounters in the text. The learner projects something onto the text from her horizon, and the text offers the interpreter something that may differ from what the interpreter initially thought the text meant to say. Heidegger and Gadamer distinguish between the first hermeneutical circle, which reflects the dynamic of parts and whole as data gradually provided by the text to the reader, and the second hermeneutical circle, which refers to the dynamic that takes place between the reader and the text's horizon, leading to a fusion of horizons.

13   "To understand a text is to follow its movement from sense to reference: from what it says, to what it talks about" (Paul Ricoeur, *Interpretation Theory: Discourse and the Surplus of Meaning* [Fort Worth: Texas Christian University Press, 1976], 87–88). On the role of metaphors in educational thinking, see Footnote 40.

a "way of looking at things."[14] This concept applies to fiction, poetry, and literary texts that address reality in an indirect way. Thus, interpreting the text does not necessarily consist of deciphering the author's intention, but rather of uncovering a perspective that is projected onto and through the text.

Gadamer's and Ricoeur's views largely fit in with twentieth-century literary criticism, which refutes the fallacy of identifying the meaning of the text with the author's intention.[15] Instead, a text establishes its own form of discourse as soon as it is written, offering something to be appropriated by the reader. This is detached from the author's intention, since written discourse immediately becomes both decontextualized from its historical setting and depsychologized from its author.[16] To interpret a text, Ricoeur asserts, is

> To seek in the text itself, on the one hand, the internal dynamic that governs the structuring of the work and, on the other hand, the power that the work possesses to project itself outside itself and to give birth to a world that would truly be the "thing" referred to by the text.[17]

---

[14] Ricoeur, *Interpretation Theory*, 92. According to Ricoeur, texts refer to reality, not only to their internal structure as claimed by New Criticism. What must be interpreted in a text is "a proposed world which I could inhabit and wherein I could project one of my ownmost possibilities" (Paul Ricoeur, *Hermeneutics and the Human Sciences* [Cambridge: Cambridge University Press, 1981], 142). His use of the term "world" of the text amplifies Gadamer's use of "the text's horizon." For the use of Ricoeur's categories of "work" and "world" in regard to the study of Hasidic* homilies, see Elie Holzer, "'Sfat Emet' Homilies in the light of Paul Ricoeur's 'work of the text,'" *Da'aT, a Journal of Jewish Philosophy and Kabbalah* (forthcoming).

[15] Leland Ryken, "Formalist and Archetypal Criticism," in *Contemporary Literary Theory: A Christian Appraisal*, ed. Clarence Walhout and Leland Ryken (Grand Rapids, MI: Eerdmans Publishing Co., 1991), 6.

[16] This does not imply an incoherent notion of an authorless text. The tie with the author is not abolished "but distended and complicated" (Ricoeur, *Hermeneutics and the Human Sciences*, 201). Ricoeur's assertion about written language and meaning is rooted in philosophical traditions. See, for example, Ricoeur, *Interpretation Theory*, and Hans-Georg Gadamer, *Truth and Method*.

[17] Ricoeur, *Hermeneutics and the Human Sciences*, 17–18.

In other words, the task of textual interpretation is to have the world of the text — its meaning — emerge through the work of the text. New connections, interpretations, and appropriations of meaning are then produced through a reciprocal interaction between reader and text.[18] However, this notion of textual autonomy and the reader's projections onto the text does not give the reader *carte blanche* to bend interpretation in any direction she wishes.[19] Rather, the text imposes limits on the scope of legitimate interpretation.[20]

This philosophical tradition is the basis of this book's close readings of rabbinic texts, as well as is its author's premise for engaging educators in the study of such texts. The basic rationale resides in what Gadamer refers to as the *awakening* role of

---

[18] Wolfgang Iser contends that the process of interpretation generates difference and that interpretation is performative in character. It makes something happen, and what arises out of this performance are emergent phenomena: "Whenever interpretation occurs, something emerges, and this something is identical neither with the subject matter nor with the register into which the subject-matter is to be transposed" (Wolfgang Iser, *The Range of Interpretation* [New York: Columbia University Press, 2000], 15). See also, Umberto Eco, *The Role of the Reader- Exploration in the Semiotics of Texts* (Bloomington: Indiana University Press, 1979).

[19] "Here is something for your consideration: a shallow person reads a profound text and says it's shallow. A profound person reads a shallow text and says that it's shallow. A shallow person reads a shallow text and says that it's profound. A profound person reads a profound text and says that it's profound. Note that the shallow person always gets it wrong, whereas the profound person always gets it right. In fact, the profound person may well err, too, but this would only happen because good reading is, among other things, an act of generosity. In other words, it is entirely possible for a profound person to see a shallow text as profound by seeing in it more than it contains, by seeing in it things that are not in it" (Steven C. Scheer, *Dancing with the Daffodils: Essays on Life and Love and Letters* [USA: Bird Brain Publishing, 2011], 5).

[20] There are three major reasons for the phenomenon of multiple interpretations. First, it is a natural outcome of the polysemic nature of written language; see Ricoeur, *Interpretation Theory*. Second, every interpretation is also impacted by the historical, limited, and changing horizons of the interpreter; see Gadamer, *Truth and Method*. Finally, reading and interpreting is a performative activity in which the reader fills gaps in the text; see Wolfgang Iser, *The Act of Reading — A Theory of Aesthetic Response* (Baltimore: Johns Hopkins University Press, 1978).

hermeneutic study of ancient texts.[21] As Hans Jauss explains, every reader brings to the text a *horizon of expectation*, the reader's finite viewpoint based on her attitudes and experiences and situated in time and history.[22] Ancient texts, which may have emerged out of the same original culture as our own but at different times and in different environments, can offer a norm or a view that challenges the present, or at least can help the reader become aware of the patterns and the limitations of her own cultural horizons. In the hermeneutic encounter with text, and with ancient traditionary texts in particular, the reader's prejudices are "being put at risk"; they are provoked and made visible so that they might eventually be revisited.[23] In other words, because of the differences in cultural-temporal horizons, these texts have the potential to reveal and prompt readers to examine their own preconceptions and to help them distinguish between those that are productive and those that are unproductive or counterproductive.[24]

---

[21]   Gadamer, *Truth and Method.*

[22]   Hans Robert Jauss, *Toward an Aesthetic of Reception* (Minneapolis: University of Minnesota, 1982).

[23]   Gadamer, *Truth and Method,* 298–299 and 388. According to Ricoeur, similar transformation will take place only through a longer process of interpretation, implying first the explanation of the text, then understanding, and finally self-understanding: "If the reference of the text is the projection of a world, then it is not in the first instance the reader who projects himself. The reader is rather broadened in his capacity to project himself by receiving a new mode of being from the text itself" (Ricoeur, *Hermeneutics and the Human Sciences,* 192). My work on *chavruta* text study builds on some of Ricoeur's conceptual distinctions. See Holzer with Kent, *A Philosophy of Havruta,* 38 n. 8 and 167–183. "Interpretation is the process by which disclosure of new modes of being—or if you prefer Wittgenstein to Heidegger, of new forms of life—gives to the subject a new capacity for knowing himself. If the reference of the text is the projection of a world, then it is not the reader who primarily projects himself. The reader rather is enlarged in this capacity of self-projection by receiving a new mode of being from the text itself" (Ricoeur, *Interpretation Theory,* 94).

[24]   This dynamic is based on Gadamer's broad concept of interpretive distance, which characterizes the human experience of understanding as a polarity. Thus, people experience tradition as something they are familiar with and yet, at the same time, as something strange or alien (Gadamer, *Truth and Method,* 295). The study of traditional texts in contemporary settings embodies this

It is in this respect that the study of ancient rabbinic texts is instrumental in the growth of contemporary educators. More specifically, the interpretive encounter with texts can move the reader in two directions: a backward direction, in making her aware of some of her own prejudices, and a forward direction, in causing her to deepen, expand, or alter her own view of the topic.[25] The educator who studies ancient texts does not seek to assimilate the historical ideas within her own horizon from the outset. Such an effort would subsume the "other" of the historical texts into the educator's own voice and convert what ought to be a *dia*logue into a monologue. It would preserve her initial presuppositions and thus forestall further thinking, introspection, and examination. According to philosophical hermeneutics, thinking and learning occur through recognition of disagreement with—or at least challenges to—one's understanding. Thus, it is by bringing out this tension between the text and the present—the reality of the reader—that this new understanding occurs. It is in this kind of dynamic that what Nicholas Davey calls *disruptive experiences* can occur, offering the reader an opportunity to change and be changed.[26]

---

play between familiarity and strangeness, leading me to select ancient Jewish texts as educational resources.

[25] Tradition and temporal distance have an effect on the actual process of understanding, described by Gadamer as *effective-history*. He characterizes historical consciousness as culminating in this kind of readiness for experience (Gadamer, *Truth and Method*, 362).

[26] Nicholas Davey, *Unquiet Understanding: Gadamer's Philosophical Hermeneutics* (Albany, NY: State University of New York Press, 2006), 7. This term echoes John Dewey's "felt difficulty," without which no learning can occur. Davey adds that, such interpretive understanding is "born of an ethical encounter with an Other, an encounter that leads to the participating subjects coming to think in different and unexpected ways of their positions" (22). Gadamer's approach to prejudices in understanding is part of a broader epistemological philosophy and a critique on modern criticism on authority. Both are beyond the scope of this chapter to be discussed. See Holzer with Kent, *A Philosophy of Havruta*, 34–59, 167–183. See also Gadamer, *Truth and Method*, 265–307.

To this end, Gadamer urges the reader to relate to the "classics" as a source from the past that may still offer a model or a norm that is relevant to the present. Reading is not only a process of questioning the meaning of the text but also of allowing the text to question us.[27] What questions does the text itself suggest, and when we ask those questions, what answers does the text offer? Understanding means placing ourselves within a process in which past and present are fused, while tradition itself is the horizon within which we do our thinking. As Gadamer writes,

> Every age has to understand a transmitted text in its own way, for the text belongs to the whole tradition whose content interests the age and in which it seeks to understand itself. The real meaning of a text [. . .] is always co-determined also by the historical situation of the interpreter and hence by the totality of the objective course of history.[28]

Accordingly, turning to rabbinic texts that reflect facets of attuned learning is not a nostalgic return, but grounded in Gadamer's attempt to bring about a particular awakening when facing ancient texts: the reader comes to understand what the text says and, at the same time, comes to a new awareness of herself—in this case, of her thinking about the interactions among teacher, student, co-learners, and the subject matter.[29]

---

27   Ricoeur is more explicit in stating that a person's self-understanding is possible only through the contour of interpretive encounters with cultural artifacts such as texts: "The subject that interprets himself while interpreting signs is no longer the cogito [. . .] he is a being who discovers, by exegesis of his own life, that he is placed in being before he [. . .] possesses himself. In this way hermeneutics would discover a manner of existing which would remain from start to finish a being-interpreted" (Paul Ricoeur, *The Conflict of Interpretations* [Evanston: Northwestern University Press, 1974], 11).

28   Gadamer, *Truth and Method*, 296.

29   This book is confined to such interpretations of rabbinic texts. For examples of pedagogical devices designed to engage students in transformative interpretive encounters with texts, see Elie Holzer with Orit Kent, *A Philosophy of Havruta*.

How This Book Came to Be

This conceptualization of text study for educators' professional
growth has been in development since 1998, when I joined
the faculty of the Mandel Teacher Educators Institute (MTEI),
a program that prepares senior educators to lead professional
development for teachers in Jewish schools and institutions across
North America.[30] MTEI emphasizes learning in and from practice
and reflection.[31] Previously, I had been schooled in the study of
rabbinic literature through both traditional and modern-academic
interpretive paradigms. My colleague and friend Dr. Gail Dorph
helped me re-conceptualize the study of rabbinic educational texts
and the kind of impact such study might have on educators.[32] From
2003 through 2007, I designed and taught in the new Beit Midrash
for Teachers, an integral part of Brandeis University's Day School
Leadership through Teaching program (DeLeT). DeLeT was then
a thirteen-month, post-BA fellowship program designed to prepare
teachers for elementary grades in Jewish day schools.[33] With the

---

[30] Elie Holzer, "Conceptions of the Study of Jewish Texts in Teachers' Professional
Development," *Religious Education* 97, no. 4 (2002): 377–403; Barry W. Holtz,
Gail Z. Dorph, and Ellen B. Goldring, "Educational Leaders as Teacher
Educators: The Teacher Educator Institute—A Case from Jewish Education,"
Peabody Journal of Education 72, no. 2 (1997): 147–166; Gail Z. Dorph and
Barry W. Holtz, "Professional Development for Teachers: Why Doesn't the
Model Change?," *Journal of Jewish Education* 66, no. 2 (2000): 67–76; and Susan
Stodolsky, Gail Z. Dorph, and Sharon Feiman-Nemser, "Professional Culture
and Professional Development in Jewish Schools: Teachers' Perceptions and
Experiences," *Journal of Jewish Education* 72, no. 2 (2006): 91–108.

[31] Deborah L. Ball and David K. Cohen, "Developing Practice, Developing
Practitioners: Toward a Practice-Based Theory of Professional Education," in
Teaching as The Learning Profession: Handbook of Policy and Practice, ed. Linda
Darling-Hammond and Gary Sykes (San Francisco: Jossey-Bass, 1999), 3–32.

[32] Over time, text study and *chavruta* learning have merged together into
"*chavruta* text study," which serves not only as a learning format in this
context, but also as a practice of professional development for teachers.
See Holzer, "Conceptions of the Study of Jewish Texts in Teachers' Professional Development"; Holzer, "What Connects 'Good' Teaching, Text Study
and Hevruta Learning? A Conceptual Argument," and Holzer with Kent,
A Philosophy of Havruta, 201–207.

[33] My colleague Dr. Orit Kent joined as co-teacher in the Beit Midrash for

creative, supportive, and inspirational leadership and guidance of Prof. Sharon Feiman-Nemser, the director of the Mandel Center, the Beit Midrash Research Project was established, through which the theoretical and pedagogical aspects of this approach further unfolded.

Over the past years, I have engaged educators with such "disruptive experiences," in the context of programs in which they processed the learning experience over extended periods of time and re-engaged their educational views, beliefs, assumptions, and values in significant ways.[34] Through these programs, we first discussed the temporal-cultural distances that separate rabbinic texts on education from our present in ways that do not allow for hiding the tensions created by these distances "by attempting a naïve assimilation."[35] Rather, it brought cultural and personal tensions out that were processed both through individual reflection and group discussions.

Among different criteria, rabbinic texts are selected texts on the basis of their accessibility to readers without prior knowledge of complex legal concepts from Talmudic literature. Additionally, they

---

Teachers and as researcher in the Beit Midrash Research Project. See Sharon Feiman-Nemser, "Beit Midrash for Teachers: An Experiment in Teacher Preparation," *Journal of Jewish Education* 72, no. 3 (2006): 161–181; Holzer with Kent, *A Philosophy of Havruta*, 23–29.

[34] This refers in particular to *Melamdim*, a two-year post-bachelor teacher education program, jointly based at the Hartman Institute in Jerusalem and Tel Aviv University, which prepares its participants to teach Judaic studies in United States community day schools, and a graduate course designed for experienced teachers who study for a Masters in Jewish Education at the Jewish Theological Seminary in New York.

[35] Gadamer, *Truth and Method*, 306. Three of such historical differences are: The ideas about teaching and learning in rabbinic texts are expressed by elite scholars. Also, they reflect a context in which the study of Torah is a religious duty and a process designed to enhance one's moral and spiritual quality of life. In addition, Torah study is conducted in settings where close and intense relationships between teachers and learners prevail. In contrast, modern educational systems have become a central institution in the wider political realm; they are rooted in liberal, democratic, and secular views of knowledge, they embrace the value of human autonomy, and they are destined for the public at large.

are usually short, allowing for a comprehensive study of the text in a relative short period of time. They also often have a strongly evocative nature; while they often seem to offer a straightforward meaning, participants discover through repeated readings that the text is more complex than it first seemed and lends itself to more than one interpretation. The literary qualities of the genre and the need to investigate the text further are particularly conducive in eliciting this kind of exploration. It is also understood that these rabbinic texts did not seek to articulate comprehensive educational views. Like sparks, they illuminate only incisive insights about teaching and learning while the educators are immersed to various degrees in highly specialized modern educational discourse, infused by psychology, sociology, epistemology, and pedagogy. Thus, rather than reaching practical conclusions, this studying is first and foremost to allow the tensions created by the ideas of these texts to affect the participants' identities as educators, without regard to any short term outcomes.[36]

Slowly, the theme of attuned learning emerged from a number of texts studied in these programs. This book discusses the fruits of this process and provides the reader with insights for her own personal

---

[36]   In a different model of Jewish educational philosophy, comprehensive works of Jewish philosophers serve as resources for systematic "educational translations." See William K. Frankena, "A Model for Analyzing a Philosophy of Education," in *Readings in the Philosophy of Education: A Study of Curriculum,* ed. Jane R. Martin (Boston: Allyn and Bacon, 1970), 15–22; Seymour Fox, Israel Scheffler, and Daniel Marom, *Visions of Jewish Education* (UK: Cambridge University Press, 2003); and Cohen and Holzer, *Modes of Educational Translation; Studies in Jewish Education.* In contrast, both the non-philosophical discursive forms of rabbinic texts and a practice-oriented approach of professional development invite the model as discussed here. It is grounded in concepts of meaning and understanding from the school of hermeneutic phenomenology and thus offers an epistemological alternative to the mere rationalistic assumptions of other models of educational translation. It is beyond the scope of this book to offer a critical comparison of the two approaches. Michael Fishbane's work reflects a groundbreaking hermeneutical theology, grounded in Jewish traditions of reading, and thus offers a similar practice-oriented philosophy of Jewish learning (Fishbane, *Sacred Attunement*). For a discussion of the educational translation of Fishbane's work, see Daniel Marom, "Educational Implications of Michael Fishbane's *Sacred Attunement*: A Jewish Theology," *Journal of Jewish Education* 74 (2008): 29–51.

exploration. It should be noted that the book does not attempt to provide a full and comprehensive account of rabbinic culture as it reflects on attuned learning. Rabbinic culture is composed of multiple—and often competing—views, beliefs, and approaches. Matters of education are no exception, and such expansive research would be far beyond the scope of a single volume. It does not document the personal journeys of students who participated in these programs, nor attempt to translate its concepts into concrete educational practices or to discuss them vis-à-vis specific ages of students. As Alberto Manguel writes,

> For these cultures of the Book, knowledge lies not in the accumulation of texts or information, nor in the object of the book itself, but in the experience rescued from the page and transformed again into experience, in the words reflected both in the outside world and in the reader's own being.[37]

This book uses several features to facilitate a similar process for its readers. Five chapters conclude with a section on "contemporary resonances," providing insights, comments, and questions that emerge by bringing the ideas of attuned learning from rabbinic texts to bear on contemporary educational practices and discourse. Footnotes are used to refer to additional resources for expanding ideas. A glossary of technical and foreign terms is provided at the end of the book.[38] Finally, the concluding chapter critically reflects on potential tensions generated through thinking about attuned learning in regard to contemporary educational and cultural contexts.

---

[37] Alberto Manguel, *The Library at Night* (New Haven: Yale University Press, 2006), 91.

[38] Terms annotated with a star (*) are elaborated in the "Glossary of Technical and Foreign Terms and Language Usage."

Modern Scholarship of Rabbinics and Education

This book incorporates methodologies developed in modern scholarship on rabbinic literature in regard to both narrative and non-narrative midrashic texts, with the choice of particular methods dictated by the texts' literary genre.[39] Literary analysis is employed to conduct a careful examination of how ideas arise in and through the interpretive, literary, and metaphorical constitution of these texts, or in "the grayish no-man's-land between exegesis and literature" that characterizes midrashic literature, to borrow the words of David Stern.[40]

Learning has been the touchstone of Jewish culture and religion throughout the centuries. This may explain modern scholars' significant interest in examining education within rabbinic culture. Marc Hirshman, an expert in both rabbinics* and Jewish education, surveys major twentieth-century scholarly works in which historical

---

[39]   Jonah Fraenkel, *Iyunim Be'olamo Haruchani Shel Sippur Ha'aggadah* (Tel Aviv: Hakibutz Hameuchad, 1981); Jonah Fraenkel, *Darkei Ha'aggadah Vehamidrash* (Israel: Masada, Yad LeTalmud, 1991); Jonah Fraenkel, *Sippur Ha'aggadah— Achdut Shel Tochen Vetzura* (Tel Aviv: Hakibutz Hameuchad, 2001); Daniel Boyarin, *Intertextuality and the Reading of Midrash* (Bloomington: Indiana University Press, 1990); David Stern, *Midrash and Theory: Ancient Exegesis and Contemporary Literary Studies* (Evanston: Northwestern University Press, 1996); Jeffrey L. Rubenstein, *Stories of the Babylonian Talmud* (Baltimore: The Johns Hopkins University Press, 2010).

[40]   David Stern, *Midrash and Theory: Ancient Exegesis and Contemporary Literary Studies* (Evanston: Northwestern University Press, 1996), 3. Metaphors are a means of processing by which human beings make sense of the world. See H. Munby, "Metaphor in the Thinking of Teachers: An Exploratory Study," *Journal of Curriculum Studies* 18 (1986): 199. Thomas Shuell writes that "If a picture is worth 1,000 words, a metaphor is worth 1,000 pictures! For a picture provides only a static image while a metaphor provides a conceptual framework for thinking about something" (Thomas J. Shuell, "Teaching and Learning as Problem Solving," *Theory into Practice* 29 [1990]: 102). Metaphors are a rich venue of expression in educational language, particularly in regard to teacher's practice. See Stan D. Ivie, *On the Wings of Metaphor* (San Francisco: Credo Gap Press, 2003); David E. Hunt, *Beginning with Ourselves in Practice, Theory and Human Affairs* (Cambridge, MA: Brookline Book, 1987); F. Michael Connely and D. Jean Clandinin, *Teachers as Curriculum Planners: Narratives of Experience* (New York: Teachers College Press, 1988). They also add clarity to complex ideas; see Eugene Provenzo et al., "Metaphor and Meaning in the Language of Teachers," *Teacher College Record* 90 (1989): 551.

and sociocultural methodologies have been used to examine the historical shifts, institutional developments, and evolving cultural norms of education in late-antique and medieval rabbinic Judaism. He combines these approaches in the analysis of legal and non-legal discussions (*sugyot**) to bring forth educational ideals such as the value of *chavruta* (paired) learning and the social mechanisms that engendered this learning culture.[41]

Published anthologies on various aspects of Jewish education have presented relevant sources from various historical periods and rabbinic works.[42] Scholars such as Admiel Kosman and Jeffrey Rubenstein use literary methods to analyze *midrash aggadah** (rabbinic legends) as a window into self-reflective and self-critical views of rabbinic learning culture, and Susan Handelman uses them to study the relationships of master and disciple through the case of Rabbi Eliezer the son of Hyrcanus.[43]

Through a close reading of one legend and a selection of short midrashic sayings that reflect aspects of attuned learning, this book uncovers insights and values that rabbinic culture has yielded in terms of the cognitive, psychological, and moral aspects of learning interactions, and explores normative elements of teachers' and learners' self-awareness vis-à-vis their modes of interaction during teaching and learning. When appropriate, the analysis of these primary texts is supplemented with parallel and/or later midrashic,

---

[41]   Marc Hirshman, *The Stabilization of Rabbinic Culture, 100 CE–350 CE: Texts on Education and Their Late Antique Context* (Oxford: Oxford University Press, 2009).

[42]   Simha Assaf and Shmuel Glick, eds., *Mekorot Letoldot Hachinuch Hayehudi* (New York: Beit Hamidrash Lerabbanim, 2001). See also Moses Aberbach, "The Relations Between Master and Disciple in the Talmudic Age," in *Essays Presented to Chief Rabbi Israel Brodie*, ed. Hirsch Jakob Zimmels, Joseph Rabbinowitz, and Israel Finestein (London: Soncino Press, 1967), 1–24; Yaakov Elman and Israel Gershoni, *Transmitting Jewish Traditions: Orality, Textuality and Cultural Diffusion* (New Haven and London: Yale University Press, 2000).

[43]   Admiel Kosman, *Massekhet Gvarim: Rav Vehakatzav Veod Sippurim* (Jerusalem: Keter Pub., 2002); Rubenstein, *Stories of the Babylonian Talmud*; Susan Handelman, *Make Yourself a Teacher: Rabbinic Tales of Mentors and Disciples* (Seattle and London: University of Washington Press, 2011).

medieval, and early-modern rabbinic texts that reflect a concern with attuned learning.

Finally, two notes are warranted in regard to the modes of reading adopted in this work. The book regularly refers to the text, the text's author(s), and the reader. The rabbinic texts' representational and expressive content issue from human experiences, intentions, and conceptions, and they reflect some consciousness. Thus, even if we could know who the authors of these texts are, what matters is the authorial presence, which animates the texts as a whole, rather than the authors' individual personalities. In the spirit of Ricoeur, the focus is on the ideas that are embodied in the text and what the text requires of the reader, through the use of its own codifications; the "intentions" of the text do not refer to the authors' conscious intentions but to those that can be detected through a careful reading of the text.

The authors of exegetical rabbinic literature seem to be aware that earlier texts appeal to the reader and, likewise, that the reader expects these texts to teach her something.[44] Thus, in the texts discussed throughout this book, ancient sages refer to biblical passages, which are part of their own cultural environment, and through them express an awareness—and encourage the cultivation—of norms and standards for interactions among learners and teachers. Similarly, these texts not only reflect educational insights but also, by design, elicit the reader's feelings, stimulate her thinking, raise her awareness, and cultivate modes of behavior in learning interactions by readers who happen to be teachers, students, and co-learners.

***

Michael Oakshott conveys the open and dynamic character that also is reflected in both the content and the structure of this book. According to Oakshott, to be truly human, individuals must claim, appropriate, and then dwell in the rich heritage of their culture— a world of meanings, not of things. Entering this world "is the only

---

[44]   David Banon, *La Lecture Infinie: Les Voies de l'Interpretation Midrashique* (Paris: Du Seuil, 1987).

way of becoming a human being, and to inhabit it is to be a human being."[45] In this work of becoming human, individuals learn to engage in conversation with their inheritance and its many voices— what Oakshott calls its various modes of thought or distinct idioms of human self-understanding. These voices reflect humanity's achievements in science, literature, the arts, politics, economics, and philosophy.

> Learning to read or to listen is a slow and exacting engagement, having little or nothing to do with acquiring information. It is learning to follow, to understand and to rethink deliberate expressions of rational consciousness; it is learning to recognize fine shades of meaning without overbalancing into the lunacy of "decoding"; it is allowing another's thoughts to reenact themselves in one's own mind; it is learning in acts of constantly surprised attention to submit to, to understand and to respond to what (in this response) becomes a part of our understanding of ourselves.[46]

---

[45]   Michael Oakshott, *The Voice of Liberal Learning: Michael Oakeshott on Education* (New Haven: Yale University Press, 1989), 45.

[46]   Ibid., 69.

Part Two

Co-Learners' Attuned Learning

Introduction

COLLABORATIVE LEARNING IN RABBINIC LITERATURE

> Just as fire cannot be made to burn with one piece
> of wood alone, so too the words of Torah cannot be
> retained by someone who studies alone.
>
> —*Babylonian Talmud, Tractate Ta'anit 7a*

Far beyond the scope of a typical class or lecture, collaborative
and argumentative learning engage two or more learners in joint
reading, text analysis, discussion, interpretation, argumentation,
and reciprocal challenging. Much rabbinic literature is interpretive
and argumentative; in fact, the Talmud* is edited as a transcription
of debates.[1] It preserves earlier competing opinions and generates
new ones through interpretation and analysis of pre-existing texts.
Thus, the very texture of the Talmud highlights the centrality
of argumentation,[2] which is at the core of the culture of Jewish
learning, and which continues to influence learning today—in both
traditional and, to a lesser extent, nontraditional formats.[3]

---

[1] Talmud, Tractate Kiddushin 30a; Maimonides, *The Laws of Torah Study.
Mishneh Torah* (Jerusalem: Yerushalem Pub., 1970), 1: 3. *Chavruta*, or paired
learning, is viewed as commonplace in studying these texts. For a review
of scholarly literature on *chavruta* learning, see Elie Holzer and Orit Kent,
"Havruta Learning: What Do We Know and What Can We Hope to Learn?," in
International Handbook on Jewish Education Vol. 1, ed. Helena Miller, Lisa Grant,
and Alex Pomson (New York: Springer, 2011), 407–418. For a contemporary
conceptualization of *chavruta* learning in light of modern theories of
interpretation and learning, see Holzer with Kent, *A Philosophy of Havruta*.

[2] This holds true even if, as some scholars believe, they are literary constructs
rather than historically accurate renditions.

[3] Simha Assaf, *Mekorot Letoldot Hachinuch Beyisrael: A Source-Book for the History*

The Advantages of Collaborative Learning

Though it is not their overt focus, a number of rabbinic texts encourage collaborative learning for all who seek Torah knowledge.[4] For example, the Babylonian Talmud instructs, "Make yourselves into groups to study the Torah, since the knowledge of the Torah can be acquired only in association with others."[5] Elsewhere it interprets the biblical term "the masters of assemblies" (Ecclesiastes 12:11) as referring to the sages* "who sit in manifold assemblies and occupy themselves with Torah," studying the law for the purpose of practical halachic* ruling.[6] More specifically, Talmudic texts ascribe benefits to collaborative learning, such as better understanding by the individual[7] and improved memorization. ("Just as fire cannot be made to burn with one piece of wood alone, so too the words of Torah cannot be retained by someone who studies alone").[8] Some

---

of *Jewish Education from the Beginning of the Middle Ages to the Period of the Haskalah* (Tel Aviv: Devir, 1925); Shaul Stampfer, *Lithuanian Yeshivas of the Nineteenth Century: Creating a Tradition of Learning* (Oxford: Littman Library of Jewish Civilization, 2012); Samuel C. Heilman, *The People of the Book: Drama, Fellowship, and Religion* (Chicago: University of Chicago Press, 1987); William Helmreich, *The World of the Yeshiva: An Intimate Portrait of Orthodox Jewry* (New Haven: Yale University Press, 1982).

4   My analysis of rabbinic literature does not seek to establish objective historical facts about the scope and the frequency of different modes of collaborative learning in Jewish history. Such an endeavor would require its own research methodology. As discussed in Chapter Two, my analysis seeks to be attentive to—and to conceptualize—the views and the consciousness that are reflected in rabbinic sources on this topic.

5   Talmud, Tractate Brachot 63b. *Chavurah,* the word used here to mean "group," is related to *chavruta,* which translates as "companionship" or "friendship" and is an extension of the Hebrew word *chaver,* "companion" or "friend."

6   Talmud, Tractate Chagiga 3b. The full context of this quote refers to the perceived tension between the plurality of the Sages' opinions on halachic matters and the unified and singular origin of that very same legal tradition. My distinction between "study" and "study for the purposes of halachic ruling" is not always as obvious in rabbinic literature.

7   Talmud, Tractate Ta'anit 7a. See also Bereishit Rabba, 69.2: "Just as a knife can only be sharpened against another, so a disciple of a sage* improves only through his *chaver* [learning partner]."

8   Ibid.

Talmudic sages warn that scholars who engage in solitary study will be cursed, grow foolish, and ultimately fall into sin;[9] for example, Rabbi Yossi the son of Chalafta (second century CE, Israel) calls his son ignorant because he studied alone.[10] Rabbi Yehoshua the son of Perachya (second century BCE, Israel) enjoins people to "acquire for yourself a *chaver*" — a friend — meaning, a learning colleague.[11]

Post-Talmudic sources reflect a similar orientation. According to Don Isaac Abrabanel (1437–1508, Portugal, Spain, and Italy), learners feel more comfortable seeking help from a study partner than from their teachers.[12] The Shelah Hakadosh (Rabbi Isaiah Horovitz, 1565–1630, Prague), stated that "one partner can reveal what the other is missing [. . .] since each partner is missing some knowledge; the power of their collaboration will motivate them to seek understanding and knowledge."[13] The Maharal of Prague (Rabbi Yehudah Loew the son of Bezalel, 1520–1609) placed paired learning in a broader religious anthropology and theology.[14] For the Maharal, only shared discourse enables the discovery of new and creative meaning.[15] Accordingly, articulating one's views to a study partner constitutes a mystical unification with the Torah, an ontological occurrence, whereby the learner transcends his limited human condition.[16]

---

[9] Ibid., 21a; Talmud Brachot 63b.

[10] Jerusalem Talmud, Tractate Nedarim 11a.

[11] *Ethics of the Fathers*, 1: 6.

[12] *Ethics of the Fathers*, 1: 6. See Isaac Abrabanel, *The Fathers' Inheritance* (New York: Silberman, 1953), 79–80.

[13] Isaiah Halevi Horovitz, *Shnei luchot habrit* (Warsaw: n.p., 1930), 48a.

[14] The Maharal was one of the stronger critics of the renewal of the *pilpul* approach to learning in his time. Originally, this approach emphasized sharp-witted disputation and innovative logical deductions of texts. The Maharal, however, believed that it had degenerated into sophistry, leading to a culture of learning in which people attempt to impress each other at the expense of the pursuit of truth, by using presupposed conclusions and unlikely interpretations of texts.

[15] For a discussion of the term "Torah study," see the Introduction to Part Three.

[16] Maharal, "Netiv HaTorah," in *Netivot Olam* (Bnei Brak: Sifrei Yehadut Ltd.,

Conceptualizations of *Machloket*

Machloket is a hallmark of rabbinic literature. The term may be translated as "dispute," "controversy," or "clash of ideas," and it encompasses opposing traditions, views, opinions, and interpretations within ancient legal-religious tradition and the subsequent disputes and debates that they engendered. *Machloket* refers to the very existence of differing views as well as to the process of argumentation. In its second meaning, the term refers to a semiotic activity involving justification, rhetorical or dialectic persuasion, and logical demonstration of a point of view.[17] At its best, this face-to-face engagement aims to arrive at compelling understanding(s) of the tradition through reciprocal argumentation. Rabbinic literature is cognizant of the potential for condemnable motives as well as of *"machloket* for the sake of heaven," namely a dispute that involves no ego, and is purely in pursuit of truth.[18]

Talmudic and post-Talmudic literature grapple with *machloket.* The very existence of multiple legal renderings challenges the halachic system. How can more than one interpretation be valid if halacha* originated from a divine source? To what extent, if at all, can autonomous human understanding and practical inferences coexist with the revealed law? What constitutes authentic and/or authoritative halachic ruling? Avi Sagi exposes this reality in his seminal work, *The Open Canon: On the Meaning of Halachic Discourse.* He provides a comprehensive map of the views and theories on the theological, hermeneutical, and ontological meaning of *machloket*

1984), 49. See also Maharal, *Derech Chaim* (Bnei Brak: Sifrei Yehadut Ltd., 1984), 297, and his comment on the importance to "cleave to learning partners."

[17]   For a historical overview of argumentation theory, see Frans H. Van Eemeren, Rob Grootendorst, and F. Snoeck Henkemans, eds., *Fundamentals of Argumentation Theory: A Handbook of Historical Backgrounds and Contemporary Developments* (Mahwah, New Jersey: Lawrence Erlbaum Associates, 1996).

[18]   See *Ethics of the Fathers* 5: 17. While this source refers to *machloket* in general, it has also been interpreted in the context of Torah study. See Norman Lamm, *Torah Lishmah: In the Works of Rabbi Hayyim of Volozhin and His Contemporaries* (New York: Yeshiva University Press, 1989), for an analysis of different meanings attributed to the expression "for the sake of heaven" in Torah study.

in the Talmudic and post-Talmudic rabbinic legal system.[19] Sagi discusses several conceptualizations of *machloket* as a positive and productive phenomenon, possibly even indispensable in the refinement of authentic halachic ruling. These theories are characterized by an *epistemological concern*, an interest in what *machloket* adds to the quality of the halachic outcome and only peripherally in its contribution to scholars' learning, comprehension, or creative interpretation.[20]

Sagi's broad analysis provides significant insights that are particularly relevant to argumentative learning. First, he points out two opposite approaches to halacha in rabbinic literature. One, a single-minded concern about the transmission of the inherited legal tradition, emphasizes breadth of knowledge, memorization, and refined comprehension. The Talmud dubs this the orientation of the "Sinai" scholar, who faithfully transmits the oral tradition believed to have been revealed along with the written Torah at Mount Sinai.[21] The second approach is *oker harim*, "uprooting mountains." Sages of this type excel in reasoning and the ability to generate new interpretive insights, thereby "uprooting" the traditions from within. Sagi shows that both orientations may embrace argumentative learning. The Sinai type will see *machloket* as a means of sharpening and improving one's understanding of the inherited tradition, whereas the sage who "uproots mountains" will see it as a legitimate avenue for creating new interpretations.[22]

---

19   Avi Sagi, *The Open Canon: On the Meaning of Halachic Discourse* (New York: Continuum, 2007).

20   As discussed by Sagi, *machloket* is conceptualized in distinct broad paradigms. Over the centuries, there have been those who saw the plurality of views as a negative reality. Others considered it as a reflection of fragmented human understanding of God's unified will. As to the dialectical learning process that this plurality engenders, some conceptualized it as a necessary means designed to retrieve the "true" meaning of the law on the basis of humans' partial understanding. Others saw it as eliciting richer but also different contingent halachic rulings, relevant to the different and contingent contexts to which they applied.

21   See Talmud, Tractate Horayot 14a, and Rashi's commentary.

22   I will draw on this distinction toward the end of my discussion in Chapter Four.

Moral Dispositions and Torah Study

Sagi's second insight relates to the potential relationship between a scholar's moral dispositions and the authenticity of a halachic ruling—its faithfulness to the legal sources and precedents, norms, and spirit of the halachic tradition.[23] In a classic passage, the Talmud addresses the issues of multiple opinions, authority, and halachic authenticity:

> Rabbi Abba stated in the name of Shmuel: For three years there was a dispute between the House of Shammai and the House of Hillel [two different academies],* with these asserting "halacha is as we say," and these contending "halacha is as we say." Then a heavenly voice announced, "These and these are [both] the words of the living God, but halacha follows the rulings of the House of Hillel." Since, however, "both are the words of the living God," why did halacha follow the rulings of the House of Hillel? Because they were kind and humble, they studied their own rulings and those of the House of Shammai, and they even cited the rulings of the House of Shammai before their own.[24]

The text recognizes that both academies' halachic views are true to tradition. To establish a legal hierarchy, the heavenly voice selects the academy of Hillel—not based on its superior expertise in Jewish law, but rather on two character traits and two corresponding behaviors. Sagi shows how post-Talmudic literature accounts for this fact. Rabbi Wolf Halevi Boskovitz (1740–1818), a leading rabbinical figure in Budapest, contends that the passage is a lesson in the religious goal of serving God. Since God values kindness and humility, the heavenly voice chooses the House of Hillel. This does not imply, however, that their kindness and humility

---

23   I am using the term "disposition" to indicate the marriage of skills and attitudes. Dispositions can be nurtured and become stable character traits through habituation to ongoing moral practices. See also Eagleton, *After Theory*, 135: "Virtue for Aristotle is not a state of mind but a disposition— which means being permanently geared for acting in a certain way even when you are not acting at all [. . .] It is that our actions create the appropriate states of mind."

24   Talmud, Tractate Eruvin 13b. See also Talmud, Tractate Gittin 6b, for other critical sources on "these and these are the words of the living God."

specifically influenced the authenticity of their halachic ruling.[25] A closer connection between moral dispositions and halachic ruling is established by the Maharal of Prague, who asserts that kindness and humility help the scholar cultivate straightforward thinking on halachic matters, eschewing unnecessary intellectual sophistication.[26] The most direct correlation between character and reliable rulings is constructed by Rabbi Haim Yossef David Azulay (1724–1806), a scholar of Jewish mysticism and history who lived in Israel and traveled across European Jewish communities. For him, humility prevents hubris by increasing a scholar's sense of uncertainty, heightening his self-criticism, and sustaining his willingness to be confronted with alternative views. He posits that these effects are central to halachic ruling and help to reduce or even eliminate erroneous legal inferences, exposing them before they become integral to the scholar's ego.[27]

These classical sources address moral dispositions as they affect learners' attitudes toward the subject matter. While building on these insights, this book focuses on attuned learning, exploring also the relevance of moral dispositions to co-learner relationships. Chapter Three analyzes texts that encourage co-learners to engage in argumentative learning and yet raise awareness regarding potential negative effects of this style of learning, such as animosity, hubris, or the clash of egos. They promote introspection and the cultivation of a complex set of psycho-social abilities, moral dispositions, and refined consciousness. Chapter Four analyzes a legend that is intended to make co-learners more aware of their expectations of collaborative learning and of the pitfalls of radically self-serving and controlling attitudes. It sets the stage for a sincere concern for the joint project of sense-making and for co-learners assisting each other in their learning process.

---

[25]   Sagi, *The Open Canon*, 105–108.

[26]   Sagi, *The Open Canon*, 116–118.

[27]   Haim Yossef David Azulay, *Petach Eynayim: Volume One* (Jerusalem: n.p., 1959), 88–89. See Sagi, *The Open Canon*, 17. See also *Ethics of the Fathers*, 6: 6 for an example of dispositions by which Torah is acquired.

Chapter Three

Self-Refinement in Argumentative Learning

> Conflict is the gadfly of thought. It stirs us to
> observation and memory. It instigates invention. It
> shocks us out of sheep-like passivity, and sets us at
> noting and contriving [. . .] [C]onflict is a "sine qua
> non" of reflection and ingenuity.
>
> —*John Dewey*[1]

Introduction

Georges B. J. Dreyfus was the first Westerner to complete the *Ge-luk* curriculum at a Tibetan Buddhist monastic college. There he learned how to engage in intense reciprocal argumentation, and upon his return to the United States, he was struck by Americans' reaction to this practice:

> My greatest disappointment in coming to an American university
> was the lack of debate. I remember at first trying to debate in
> classes with other students or with the professor, but such attempts
> usually ended badly. In one class, I was told that debating was
> not what "gentlemen" should engage in. In another, the professor
> was only too delighted to debate me in his area of specialization,
> where he obviously had the upper hand, but this made the other
> students uncomfortable. "How can you be so harsh toward
> a student?" they asked him. "Oh, don't worry. He is well trained.
> He can take it," was the reply.

As I have tried to make clear, the monastery allows for freer encounters. There, nobody is offended at being defeated in debate

---

1   John Dewey, *Human Nature and Conduct* (New York: Modern Library, 1957), 300.

or even made fun of. I find this culture of disagreement too often missing in American higher education, where students and faculties are at times overly sensitive and preoccupied with their reputations.[2]

Years later, while serving as a professor of religion at Williams College, Dreyfus came to understand that the difference in attitudes toward argumentation is cultural. Around the world and throughout history, societies have attached different levels of positive and negative value to the practice of debate. This is not a matter of absolute good or bad, however. Even societies that are supportive of argumentative learning may develop an awareness of some of its potential pitfalls, especially in the realm of human relationships, as argumentation may also nourish moral hubris, animosity, or a clash of egos. This double-edged aspect of argumentative learning caused philosophers of different ages to warn about such pitfalls while promoting argumentation. Thus Socrates (470–399 BCE), known for attributing a central role to the opposition of ideas, is quoted as saying:

> You, Gorgias, like myself, have had great experience of disputations, and you must have observed, I think, that they do not always terminate in mutual edification, or in the definition by either party of the subjects which they are discussing; but disagreements are apt to arise—somebody says that another has not spoken truly or clearly; and then they get into a passion and begin to quarrel, both parties conceiving that their opponents are arguing from personal feeling only and jealousy of themselves, not from any interest in the question at issue. And sometimes they will go on abusing one another until the company at last are quite vexed at themselves for ever listening to such fellows.[3]

Talmudic and later rabbinic disputations evince strongly held opinions and argumentative learning. As explained by Jeffrey Rubenstein, fifth- and sixth-century sages in Babylon considered dialectical and argumentative abilities indispensable for generative learning of the legal-religious tradition, and in fact considered such

---

2   Georges B. J. Dreyfus, *The Sound of Two Hands Clapping: The Education of a Tibetan Buddhist Monk* (Berkeley: University California Press, 2003), 331.

3   Plato, *Gorgias*, lines 583–591; http://classics.mit.edu/Plato/gorgias.html.

aptitudes the measure of excellence in learning. However, a number of rabbinic texts also offer an implied critique of some aspects of argumentative learning, including the possibility of personal hostility.[4]

The rabbinic texts in this chapter advocate for the cultivation of certain dispositions in and through argumentative learning, instilling a drive toward self-refinement through monitoring elusive feelings and ambiguous intentions.[5] This analysis reveals ways in which midrashic* literature blurs the differences between text and commentary, using literary techniques such as biblical proof texts, designed to impact the reader's views through new semantic meanings .[6]

The Double Edge of Argumentative Learning
(Babylonian Talmud, Tractate Shabbat 63a)

Flimsy Hook or Strong Argument?

Rabbi Yirmiya and Rabbi Elazar (fourth century CE, Israel) bring seemingly flimsy biblical proof texts to demonstrate the value and terms of argumentative learning. They cite Psalms 45:4–5:

> Gird your sword under your thigh, O hero, in your splendor and glory; in your glory as success, win success; ride on in the cause of truth and humble righteousness, and your right hand will teach you awesome things.[7]

Lacking an obvious connection to learning, this "proof text" forces the reader to engage actively and immediately with the sages' thinking:

> Rabbi Yirmiya said in Rabbi Elazar's name: When two scholars sharpen each other in [matters of] halacha, the Holy One, blessed be He, gives them success, for it is said (Psalms 45:5), "in your

---

4   Rubenstein, *Stories of the Babylonian Talmud*, 13–14.

5   For my use of the term *dispositions*, see Chapter One, Footnote 9.

6   Stern, *Midrash and Theory*.

7   חגור חרבך על ירך גבור הודך והדרך. והדרך צלח רכב על דבר אמת וענוה צדק ותורתך נוראות ימינך.

glory win success." Read not "your glory" (*vahadarcha*) but "your sharpening" (*vechadadcha*). Moreover, they ascend to greatness, as it is said, "ride on in success."

One might think [that this is so] even if it is not for its own sake; therefore it is taught, "In the cause of truth." One might think [that this is so] even if he is becoming conceited; therefore it is taught, "And humble righteousness." (Psalms 45:5)[8]

The first sentence clearly encourages reciprocal sharpening and announces its consequent benefit—a divine reward. Drawing on the authoritative biblical text then enhances the reader's confidence in the value of this norm. The odd choice of biblical proof texts, the intricacies of the midrash's interpretive work, and the semantic effects of the movement between the biblical and the midrashic texts may elicit additional insights in regard to argumentative learning. The biblical poet dedicates his words to a noble king who "rides on in success," strongly advocating the cause of truth and humble righteousness. In the midrashic teaching, this kingly figure is transformed from military hero to scholar. At the outset, these biblical verses do not relate to learners and learning, nor do the surrounding verses. First, the midrash deliberately connects reciprocal sharpening to warfare, creating a virile, if not violent, base on which to build the idea of argumentative learning.[9] Modern scholars of rabbinic literature have noted a "spiritualizing"

---

8   Talmud, Tractate Shabbat 63a.

אמר רבי ירמיה אמר רבי אלעזר: שני תלמידי חכמים המחדדין זה לזה בהלכה, הקדוש ברוך הוא מצליח להם,
שנאמר והדרך צלח. אל תקרי והדר אלא וחדדך. ולא עוד אלא שעולין לגדולה, שנאמר צלח רכב. יכול אפילו
שלא לשמה, תלמוד לומר על דבר אמת. יכול אם הגיס דעתו, תלמוד לומר וענוה צדק.

9   George Lakoff and Mark Johnsen analyze how concepts, people's activities, and language are metaphorically structured and interrelated. The first example they discuss is *argument is war*: "This is an example of what it means for a metaphorical concept [. . .] to structure (at least in part) what we do and how we understand what we are doing when we argue. *The essence of metaphor is understanding and experiencing one kind of thing in terms of another.*" The authors also suggest: "Try to imagine a culture where arguments are not viewed in terms of war [. . .] Imagine a culture where an argument is viewed as a dance" (George Lakoff and Mark Johnsen, *Metaphors We Live By* [London: The University of Chicago Press, 2003], 3–5). I thank Marc Brettler for referring me to this book.

sublimation of warfare motifs, symbols, and terminology that substitute for nonviolent ones, perhaps with the intention of distancing diaspora Jews from an activist, political, and military ethos.[10] The midrashic suggestion of *vechadadcha* (your sharpening) to replace *vahadarcha* (your glory) obscures its literal meaning. The new heroic symbol of rabbinic culture—the sage—*eclipses* the warrior/king.

Paul Ricoeur's notion of *vivid metaphor* invites a more nuanced view. For Ricoeur, at their most basic level, metaphors generate semantic innovations by creating a tension between two unrelated contexts, causing the listener or reader to see something new.[11] The midrash juxtaposes, or perhaps even merges, the earlier and later contexts of warfare and learning. The association with an extreme case of violent confrontation underscores the passionate clashing of learners' views: not a gentle exchange of ideas, but rather a dynamic in which learners fully engage and put forward their views unhesitatingly, as if their lives depend on the outcome of the argument. This is the condition needed for reciprocal sharpening, and war serves as an important rabbinic metaphor for study.[12]

---

[10]   See Aviezer Ravitzky, "HaShalom Kemusag Kosmi, Utopia Vehistoria Bahagut Hayehudit Beyemei Habeinayim," *Da'at- A Journal of Jewish Philosophy and Kabbalah* 17 (1986): 11–12; Elie Holzer, *A Double-Edged Sword: Military Activism in the Thought of Religious Zionism* (Bar Ilan University: The Faculty of Law and Shalom Hartman Institute Press, 2008), 26–27; 241–242. Daniel Boyarin and Admiel Kosman provide a similar explanation of rabbinic interpretations designed to cultivate more feminine cultural role models. See Daniel Boyarin, *Carnal Israel: Reading Sex in Talmudic Culture* (Berkeley: University of California Press, 1995); Kosman, *Massekhet Gvarim*. See Avi Sagi, "The Punishment of Amalek in Jewish Tradition: Coping with the Moral Problem," *The Harvard Theological Review* 87 (1994): 323–346, for his extended discussion on interpretive strategies used in rabbinic literature in order to neutralize violent normative biblical texts.

[11]   Paul Ricoeur, *The Rule of Metaphor—Multi-disciplinary Studies of the Creation of Meaning in Language* (Toronto, Buffalo, and London: University of Toronto Press, 1975), 65–100. For the use of metaphors as a key to educational thinking, see Chapter Two, Footnote 40.

[12]   See Gila Ratzerdorfer Rozen, "Empathy and Aggression in Torah Study: Analysis of a Talmudic Description of Havruta Learning," in *Wisdom from All*

The use of this metaphor adds another nuance. In battle, the warrior's intent is to defeat his enemy, and the abrasion—perhaps even sharpening—of the sword may occur if it happens to meet the enemy's sword on its trajectory. This is definitely an ancillary effect. On the other hand, the midrashic metaphor places abrasion at the center of the image. In their encounter, each scholar does try to advance his own views; and yet, by deemphasizing the glory of victory, the midrash turns the erstwhile side effect—the refinement, or sharpening, of each other's learning—into the primary gain of argumentative dynamic.

Generally speaking, a change in vowels is a subtle and palatable interpretive technique because vowels in written Hebrew in this time period were dictated by context, rather than being explicitly written out as the consonants were.[13] This midrash is more blatant, however; it overtly changes two consonants, literally rewriting the biblical word *vahadarcha* והדרך (and your glory) as *vechadadcha* וחדדך (and your sharpening): the *heh* (ה) is replaced by a *chet* (ח) and the *resh* (ר) is replaced by a *dalet* (ד). The semantic effect is striking: rather than reading the new word as replacing the biblical, the midrash seems to read the two words as pointing to each other.[14] Their close graphic similarity brings the two words together, as if one is layered on top of the other. This partially obliterates their different semantic contexts while conveying new meanings: the kingly aura that accompanies adversarial learning, and the king's courage as a warrior, are sublimated here in the courage that is necessary to invest oneself fully in argumentative learning.

My Teachers, ed. Jeffrey Sacks and Susan Handelman (Jerusalem and New York: Urim Publications, 2003), 249–263, for a discussion of this topic and similar sources.

13 Vowels were only explicitly written out beginning in the late first millennium CE.

14 For a late medieval conceptualization of this interpretive technique, see Maharal, *The Book of the Well of Exile* (Jerusalem: Sifrei Yehadut, 1984), 40–49. According to the Maharal, the Midrash is more interested in the semantic similarity than in the phonetic difference of words. The interpretive type of "do not read . . . but . . ." is a self-conscious invitation to stray from the text's literal meaning and bring in ideas through word play.

In addition, the image of the sharpened sword emphasizes the value of encountering alternative views. Mere exposure to different opinions is not likely to alter one's views; change takes place through uninhibited engagement. Furthermore, deconstructing a learning partner's position requires being open to change as well — in the image, both irons are sharpened. In this differential space, and in the dialectical process, the differences between perspectives are disclosed and sharpened, and each learner's perspective vis-à-vis the given topic is enriched and transformed.[15]

Intrapersonal Dispositions in Argumentative Learning

The midrash tempers this bellicose brand of learning by offering two disclaimers. The first is about desirable dispositions worth cultivating. It is structured in a typical midrashic formula as follows:

The Midrash	Structural Explanation
One might think [that this is so]	The midrash explicates a first potential misinterpretation of the exhorted practice, namely
even if it is not for its own sake;	that it is independent of the learner's improper motivation
therefore it is taught, "in the cause of truth."	and confines its exhortation to the learner's striving for truth.

The rhetorical statement "one might think" rules out a likely reading and brings to light something that otherwise might have remained unnoticed. The midrash thereby signals that even though it has suggested aggressiveness, argumentative learning needs to be

---

15   In the case of the Midrash, that subject matter is religious law: "two scholars sharpen each other in halacha." See Holzer with Kent, *A Philosophy of Havruta*, 190. This view of learning reflects broader philosophical ideas, especially in the context of the tradition of philosophical hermeneutics.

regulated by ongoing, two-tiered self-refinement. Whereas the goal in warfare is to defeat the enemy, in learning, the forceful exchange must be geared toward mastering the topic at hand ("in the cause of truth"). The medieval commentator Rashi (1040–1105) interprets the word *hamechadedin* (who sharpen) as "question and respond, not to subjugate but to become sharper."[16] He thereby enriches the psychological meaning of reciprocal sharpening that is "in the cause of truth": a dynamic that contributes to the learner's own understanding is distinct from one that turns into a bid for personal domination. Thus, the midrash stresses consciousness of one's own motives.[17]

A second "one might think" introduces the other disclaimer:

The Midrash	Structural Explanation
One might think [that this is so]	The midrash explicates a second potential misinterpretation of the exhorted practice, namely
even if he is becoming conceited;	that it is independent of the learner's subsequent feeling of conceit
therefore it is taught, "and humble righteousness."	and confines its exhortation to the humble learner.*

* יכול אם הגיס דעתו, תלמוד לומר וענוה צדק.

---

16   In Hebrew: שואלין ומשיבין, ולא לקפח אלא כדי להתחדד.

17   See Terence I. Irwin, "Plato's Objection to the Sophists," in *The Greek World*, ed. Anton Powell (London: Routledge, 1997), 568–590. This distinction echoes the ancient Greek term "eristic," referring to the use of argumentation with the sole goal of defeating the other side or enjoying disputation for its own sake, rather than as a means to discover a truth or a probable answer to any specific question. It is an art by which people protect their beliefs or self-interests in rational dialogue and during the process of arguing. Compare with Charles Baudelaire, *Paris Spleen: Little Poems in Prose* (Middletown: Wesleyan University Press, 2010), 30. In his poem "The Cake," two children fight over a piece of bread: "The cake travelled from hand to hand, and

Arrogance may be fueled by the learner's success in argumentation, which confers a sense of superiority vis-à-vis a learning partner.[18] This negative disposition is contrasted with "humble righteousness," the potential antidote for overt complacency. The midrash offers neither a protocol nor specific instructions for neutralizing potential negative effects of argumentative learning, seemingly aware that these are a constant threat and that the only way to deal with them is through the cultivation of ongoing alertness and self-refinement. Both of these dispositions require honesty and humility, anticipating Howard Gardner's *intrapersonal intelligence*—the capacity to detect and access one's own range of emotions, and to label, assess, and use them as behavior guides.[19] However, while Gardner believes that people with high intrapersonal intelligence tend to be introverted and less socially oriented, this midrash expects learners to cultivate this kind of intrapersonal intelligence in and through the very nexus of their interactions with others.

The second-century Talmudic sage Rabbi Nechunia the son of Hakana is said to have uttered a prayer every day when entering the hall of study and before learning with others. He would pray, "May it be your will, Lord my God, God of my fathers, that I shall not be angry with my associates, and that my associates shall not be angry with me."[20] He even attributed the merit of his old age to the fact that, "I have never sought honor through the degradation of my colleagues, nor have I taken the curses of my colleagues with me to

---

changed from pocket to pocket, at every moment; but, alas, it changed also in size; and when at length, exhausted, panting and bleeding, they stopped from the sheer impossibility of going on, there was no longer any cause of feud; the slice of bread had disappeared, and lay scattered in crumbs like the grains of sand with which it was mingled."

[18]   The English translation correctly renders "is *becoming* conceited", emphasizing the process that yields arrogance.

[19]   Howard Gardner, *Frames of Mind: The Theory of Multiple Intelligences* (New York: Basic Books, 1983), 251–292.

[20]   Jerusalem Talmud, Tractate Brachot 4: 20.

my bed."[21] Rabbi Nechunia addresses negative tendencies through an intrapersonal orientation expressed through introspection, prayer, and forgiveness toward his colleagues.

An Argument for Friendship
(Babylonia Talmud, Tractate Ta'anit 7a)

Argumentative learning can yield a special type of togetherness, as the following midrash teaches:

> Iron by iron together; and a person in face-to-face togetherness with his friend (Proverbs 27:17).[22] Rabbi Chama the son of Rabbi Chanina [third century BCE, Israel] said: What is meant by writing, "Iron by iron together"? To tell you: Like this iron that sharpens the other, so two scholars sharpen each other in halacha.[23]

Neither the biblical verse nor the midrashic teaching is formulated as an obligation, and unlike the previous midrash, no explicit promises of reward is recorded. Again the biblical verse that serves as the basis of the midrashic teaching does not evoke a situation of teaching and learning, which makes the careful reader wonder why it was chosen.[24] As is often the case in the Book of Proverbs, the verse in question lacks a verb. Abrasion and sharpening are only implied by "iron by iron together," and the reader projects these verbs onto the image offered by the metaphor. Furthermore, the translation for the second half of the verse is somewhat obscure.

---

[21]   Talmud, Tractate Megillah 28a.

[22]   ברזל בברזל יחד ואיש יחד פני רעהו.

[23]   אמר רבי חמא בן רבי חנינא: מאי דכתיב ברזל בברזל יחד? לומר לך: מה ברזל זה אחד מחדד את חברו, אף שני
תלמידי חכמים מחדדים זה את זה בהלכה.

[24]   Thus, by quoting the verse "iron by iron together," the Midrash does more than just utilize the verse as a technical jumping-off point. Consider the significance of Rabbi Chama's choice of verse 17 rather than verse 19 of Proverbs, Chapter 27, which directly refers to personal interaction: "As in water, face [reflects] face, so too does the heart of a person [reflects] to the other person." The imagery of two irons scraping against each other is very different from that of verse 19, which involves a face and water that may be reflective, and certainly is not abrasive.

The word *yachad* (together) is the key to the meaning of the second part of the verse: it conjures two human beings facing each other in a moment of existential *togetherness*, which somehow mutually impacts their faces. This togetherness must be a deep, reciprocal awareness grounded in the learners' trust and care—the type of reciprocal presence that leads to mutual impact.[25]

This midrash points to a somewhat elusive dimension of learning interactions that nevertheless resonates with learners who experience it. Togetherness in the common endeavor of reciprocal sharpening is a form of friendship; it connects two learners intellectually as well as emotionally. Personal affection may or may not play a part, but mutual goodwill and a shared delight develops through analyzing and seeking to understand the subject matter. The friendship reflects a sense of community, which is, according to educational philosopher Parker Palmer, the key to the distinction between competition and conflict:

> Competition is a secretive, zero-sum game played by individuals for private gain; conflict is open and sometimes raucous but always communal, a public encounter in which it is possible for everyone to win by learning and growing. Competition is the antithesis of community, an acid that can dissolve the fabric of relationships. Conflict is the dynamic by which we test ideas in the open, in a communal effort to stretch each other and make better sense of the world.[26]

---

[25]   This understanding is similar to that of commentators such as Rashi, who paraphrases the midrash's teaching while quoting *both* parts of the biblical verse:

ברזל בברזל יחד ואיש יחד פני רעהו, מה ברזל זה אחד מחדד את חברו, כגון סכין על גבי חברתה.

"Iron (sharpens) by iron; and a man together (with) the face of his friend.— Like this iron, one sharpens its fellow (iron), as a knife on the surface of its fellow (knife)."

[26]   Parker J. Palmer, *The Courage to Teach: Exploring the Inner Landscape of a Teacher's Life* (San Francisco: Jossey-Bass Publishers, 2009), 103. Similar insights about the fellowship and friendship that are nurtured in and through the virile aspect of argumentation are expressed by late-Renaissance humanist Michel de Montaigne (1533–1592): "I like a strong, manly fellowship and familiarity, a friendship that delights in the sharpness and vigor of its intercourse, as does love in bites and scratches that draw blood. It is not vigorous and generous enough if it is not quarrelsome, if it is civilized and artful, if it fears knocks

Attuned Learning: Contemporary Resonances

Over the past two or three decades, scholars and educators have come to recognize the importance of argumentative learning. Social psychologists David Johnson and Roger Johnson champion *constructive controversy*, an instructional procedure that combines cooperative learning—working together to achieve a common educational task—with structured intellectual conflict, arguing the pros and cons of a given case and thereby stimulating problem-solving and reasoned judgment. Johnson and Johnson have monitored learners' experiences through role-playing, tasks, and procedural steps. They emphasize that "Conflict among ideas, theories, or conclusions leads to uncertainty about correctness of one's views, which leads to epistemic curiosity and the active search for additional information and perspectives, which, in turn, leads to re-conceptualized and refined conclusions."[27] They have

---

and moves with constraint. *For there can be no discussion without contradiction* (Cicero)" (Michel de Montaigne, *The Complete Works: Essays, Travel Journal, Letters*, trans. Donald M. Frame [New York, London and Toronto: Everyman's Library, 2003], 856). A similar idea is conveyed through the subtle permutations that the midrash performs on the Hebrew words, capitalizing on the grammatical principle that three-letter (and sometimes two-letter) roots may tie disparate words to a common source. In this particular case, the word "together" (*yachad*)—which appears twice in the original verse—turns into the key word inserted by Rabbi Chama, "sharpen" (*mechadedin*), from the verb "to sharpen" (*lechaded*), thanks to their shared root letters *chet* (ח) and *dalet* (ד). Again, attention is called to the connection between reciprocal sharpening in learning and a sense of authentic togetherness. Such an approach transcends a narrower view of argumentative learning which is merely interested in the individual's learning benefits.

[27] David W. Johnson and Roger T. Johnson, "Energizing Learning: The Instructional Power of Conflict," *Educational Researcher* 38 (2009): 37–51. See also David M. Donahue, "Conflict as a Constructive Curricular Strategy," in *Democratic Dilemmas of Teaching Service-Learning: Curricular Strategies for Success*, ed. Christine M. Cress, David M. Donahue, and Associates (Virginia: Stylus Publishing, LLC, 2011), 101–109. Johnson and Johnson discuss some of the benefits of conflict or argumentation in David W. Johnson and Roger T. Johnson, *Cooperation and Competition, Theory and Research* (Edina: Interaction Book Company, 1989). See also David Johnson, Roger Johnson, and Karl Smith, "Academic Controversy: Enriching College Instruction through Intellectual Conflict," *ASHE-ERIC Higher Education Report* 25 (Washington, DC: The George Washington University,

concluded that this type of learning enhances cognitive abilities, positive attitudes, and interpersonal interaction.

Educators from kindergarten through college emphasize the importance of critical thinking for the cultivation of responsible democratic citizens. This has triggered a special interest in argumentative learning, which could nurture students' confidence in their own ideas.[28] Students are given tools for questioning others' ideas and societal ideals; disagreements serve as opportunities to teach how to watch for value-laden, conflict-ridden situations.[29] As a result, the philosophy of education has shifted to highlight autonomous thinking and civilized disagreement.

The rabbinic texts in this chapter prod educators to look beyond this acquisition of critical thinking skills, rhetorical abilities, and debating techniques and, in doing so, suggest how educators may design new learning environments and teach new abilities. These rabbinic teachings awaken educators to the intrapersonal dimension of argumentative learning, in which the learner's emotions, morality, and cognition are inextricably interrelated. Unlike common practice in contemporary educational literature, these texts do not propose a set of rules or techniques. Instead, they prompt educators to cultivate the environment and opportunities students need in

---

Graduate School of Education and Human Development, 1997); David W. Johnson and Roger T. Johnson, "Energizing Learning: The Instructional Power of Conflict," *Educational Researcher* 38 (2009): 49. In their numerous publications, they describe what they call "constructive controversy," a pedagogical approach that takes advantage of the constructive features of engaging in conflict. This approach asks participants to explore the advantages and disadvantages of particular ideas with the aim of reaching a new synthesis. In the current context, I do not posit that the goal is always synthesis.

[28]   James Arthur, Ian Davies, and Carole Hahn, eds., *SAGE Handbook of Education for Citizenship and Democracy* (Thousand Oaks: Sage Publications, 2008).

[29]   See Deborah Meier, *The Power of Their Ideas* (Boston: Beacon, 1995) and her five "habits of mind" necessary to become both a powerful and well-informed citizen. See also Deborah Meier, "Supposing that . . .," *Phi Delta Kappan* 78 (1996): 276. She writes that whether a child grows up to become a cosmologist or a cosmetician, "both need to know how to think about complex matters, both need to care about others, and both need to know how to learn new things to keep up vocationally."

order to learn how to call upon their mental, emotional, and moral resources during argumentative learning, while maintaining an honest quest for understanding. Growing into the type of attuned learner reflected in these rabbinic texts means honing a complex array of abilities involving self-knowledge and refined consciousness.[30] Critical self-awareness points to a process of personal growth including the ability to identify and modulate one's own attitudes rather than being entirely subject to them.[31] This approach offers an opportunity to think past dichotomous educational views, with radical separations—between means and ends, between pedagogy and goals, between learning as an intellectual and as an existential activity, and between the instrumental and the ethical-formative dimensions of learning. By emphasizing the formative aspect reflected in the rabbinic texts, educators can convey an element of morality that is embedded in argumentative learning. Drawing out elements of attuned learning leads to an emphasis on the learner as an individual and the relationship between how she learns and the type of human being she strives to be.[32] These texts challenge contemporary educators and learners to explore a more holistic outlook, in which positive habits of the heart and positive habits of the mind are fostered simultaneously.

---

[30]   See David Carr, "Rival Conceptions of Practice in Education and Teaching," *Journal of Philosophy of Education* 37 (2003): 253–266. This view of education is grounded in Jewish and neo-Aristotelian views of ethics and of learning, in which it is assumed that one's interiority and actions are intertwined and impact one another. Aristotle's concept of the virtuous person is significant in this regard: someone who consciously and knowingly chooses virtuous action, and has the disposition to accomplish that action. See Dunne, *Back to the Rough Ground* and his discussion of the neo-Aristotelian tradition in the context of education.

[31]   Rodgers and Raider-Roth, "Presence in Teaching," 271; Robert Kegan, *The Evolving Self* (Cambridge, MA: Harvard University Press, 1982); Robert Kegan, *In Over Our Heads: The Mental Demands of Modern Life* (Cambridge, MA: Harvard University Press, 1994).

[32]   See Holzer with Kent, *A Philosophy of Havruta*, 200: collaborative learning can be said to be a humanizing activity. See also George Steiner, *Real Presences* (Chicago: University of Chicago Press, 1991).

Chapter Four

Study Partners' Learning

> In genuine dialogue the turning to the partner takes place in all truth, that is, it is a turning of the being. Every speaker "means" the partner or partners to whom he turns as this personal existence. To "mean" someone in this connection is at the same time to exercise that degree of making present which is possible to the speaker at that moment [. . .] Of course such an acceptance does not mean approval; but no matter in what way I am against the other, by accepting him as my partner in genuine dialogue I have affirmed him as a person.
>
> —*Martin Buber*[1]

> Attention to each other is a form of acceptance
>
> —*R. Zadok Hacohen of Lublin*[2]

Introduction

Oscar Wilde, through his nineteenth-century short story character, foreshadows a contemporary cultural phenomenon: "'You are a very irritating person,' said the Rocket, 'and very ill bred. I hate people who talk about themselves, as you do, when one wants to talk about oneself, as I do.'"[3]

Today, sociologist Charles Derber calls this *conversational narcissism*. These "ways conversationalists act to turn the topics of

---

[1]   Martin Buber, "Elements of the Interhuman," in *The Knowledge of Man; Selected Essays,* ed. Maurice Friedman (Baltimore: Humanity Books, 1988), 75–76.

[2]   Rabbi Zadok Hacohen, *Tzidkat Hatzadik* (Bnei Brak: Brody Katz, 1973), 69.

[3]   Oscar Wilde, *The Complete Fairy Tales of Oscar Wilde* (Digireads.com Publishing, 2006), 29.

ordinary conversations to themselves without showing sustained interest in others' topics" have arisen with modern individualism.[4] Cultural historian Christopher Lasch points to "the culture of competitive individualism," which lends itself to egocentrism in education both in and outside of the classroom. These relationships are "bland, superficial and deeply unsatisfying" and are characterized by a lack of commitment.[5]

The challenge of human interaction stretches beyond these modern individualistic norms.[6] Teachers, students, and co-learners have always been vulnerable to such pitfalls due to social status, unarticulated assumptions, and unconscious roles. Norms involving the forms and purposes of communication often remain implicit: they are embedded in natural conversational patterns and remain unnoticed until one of the participants questions them outright.[7] The legend of Rabbi Yochanan and Resh Lakish (Rabbi Shimon the son of Lakish, third century CE, Israel) at the center of this chapter has nurtured important reflections on key issues including rabbinic authority, rabbi-student relationships, and collaborative learning.[8]

---

[4]   Charles Derber, *The Pursuit of Attention: Power and Individualism in Everyday Life* (Oxford: Oxford University Press, 1979), 25.

[5]   Christopher Lasch, *The Culture of Narcissism: American Life in an Age of Diminishing Expectations* (New York: Basic Books, 1978), 40. See Robert N. Bellah, Richard Madsen, William M. Sullivan, Ann Swidler, and Steven M. Tipton, *Habits of the Heart: Individualism and Commitment in American Life* (New York: Harper & Row, 1985) for a broader view of individualism as a central characteristic of modernity that replaces tradition and community.

[6]   Erich Fromm emphasizes the primacy of individualism and its impact on egoism in modern capitalist cultures: Erich Fromm, *Escape from Freedom* (New York: Avon, 1941). Emile Durkheim sees in egoism a response to the weakening of traditional social bonds: Emile Durkheim, *Suicide* (New York: Free Press, 1951).

[7]   Jurgen Habermas, *The Theory of Communicative Action* (Boston: Beacon, 1984); Karl-Otto Apel, "The Problem of Philosophical Foundations in Light of a Transcendental Pragmatics of Language," in *After Philosophy: End or Transformation?*, ed. Kenneth Baynes, James Bohman, and Thomas McCarthy (Cambridge, MA: MIT Press, 1987), 250–290. For these philosophers, it is both important and helpful to make a set of such norms visible and explicit.

[8]   See Elie Wiesel, "Rabbi Johanan and Resh Lakish," in *Alei Shefer; Studies in the Literature of Jewish Thought, Presented to Rabbi Dr. Alexandre Safran,*

A close reading shows that the legend is designed to subtly raise co-learners' awareness of conversational narcissism and the necessity of taking care of each other's learning.

Some Talmudic legends (*aggadot*, in Hebrew) utilize carefully designed literary devices to draw attention to potential conflicts, existential dilemmas, and tensions. They even implicitly criticize their own culture's highest value—Torah study—without undermining its primacy. Jonah Fraenkel points out that rabbinic legends, in contrast to lyrical stories, pay little explicit attention to the characters' emotions.[9] Fraenkel also stresses the "internal self-containedness" of these pieces, which provide all necessary information to convey the intended message. Yet, as Jeffrey Rubenstein posits, a legend's sufficiency need not preclude enhanced understanding through connections with other legends or other Talmudic texts involving similar characters or themes.[10]

Perceptions of Learning Partnerships
(Babylonian Talmud, Tractate Baba Metzia 84a—84b and Tractate Shabbat 63a)

Verbal learning interactions reflect fundamental assumptions about the nature of inquiry and of communication, about knowledge,

---

ed. Mosheh Hallamish (Ramat-Gan: Bar-Ilan University Press, 1990), 175–194; Boyarin, *Carnal Israel*, 215–219; Fraenkel, *Iyounim Beolamo Haruchani Shel Sippur Haaggadah*, 74–78; Ruth Calderon, *Hashuk. Habayit. Halev* (Jerusalem: Keter Publishing, 2001), 27–40; Admiel Kosman, *Massekhet Gvarim: Rav Vehakatzav Veod Sippurim* (Jerusalem: Keter Publishing 2002), 34–51; Yehuda Liebes, "Eros Ve'anti Eros al Hayarden," in *Life as a Sanctuary: Studies in Jewish Psychology*, ed. Schachar Arazi, Michal Fachler, and Baruch Kahana (Tel Aviv: Yediot Acharonot Publishing, 2004), 157–162. Of these scholars, only Kosman (to some extent) frames the story as being essentially about collaborative learning.

9   Fraenkel, *Darkei Haaggada Vehamidrash.*

10   Jeffrey L. Rubenstein, *Talmudic Stories: Narrative Art, Composition and Culture* (Baltimore and London: The Johns Hopkins University Press, 2003).

and about the roles to be assumed by the participants.[11] In rabbinic literature, the learning relationship of Rabbi Yochanan and Resh Lakish has been viewed over the centuries as a successful, ideal model.[12] The two sages' idealized conversational learning patterns are contrasted with the poor learning dynamic that takes place between Rabbi Yochanan and another sage, Rabbi Elazar:[13]

> Rabbi Shimon the son of Lakish died, and Rabbi Yochanan was greatly distressed over Resh Lakish's death. The sages said, "Who will go and relieve his mind?" They [the other sages in the Talmudic academy] decided to let Rabbi Elazar the son of Pedat go, for his statements were sharply formulated [and his acumen might serve as a satisfactory substitute for that of Resh Lakish].[14] Rabbi Elazar went and sat before Rabbi Yochanan. After

---

11   Nicholas C. Burbules and Bertram C. Bruce, "Theory and Research on Teaching as Dialogue," in *Handbook of Research on Teaching 4th Edition*, ed. Virginia Richardson (Washington, DC: American Educational Research Association, 2001), 1102–1121.

12   Talmudic literature places both in Israel-Palestine in the second half of the second century CE. Rabbi Yochanan is introduced as the head of the leading Talmudic academy of his time. Interpretations of this text as the model of a successful learning relationship are in various literary genres such as sixteenth-to-seventeenth-century Talmudist Shmuel Idelsh's commentary and nineteenth-century Hasidic master Rabbi Mordechai Yosef Leiner of Izbica's book, *Mei Shiloach*. Addressing Genesis 2:18, "I will make him a helpmate for him" (*ezer kenegdo*, literally, "a help against him"), Rabbi Leiner comments: "This is the Creator's will, that a person will grow and be helped by someone who is opposed to him. Like a student and a teacher, as we found about Resh Lakish against Rabbi Yochanan, who used to ask him twenty-four questions, and the latter responded twenty-four answers, and thus the subject would be clarified/expanded. And not like Rabbi Elazar, who kept saying, 'There is a *baraita* supporting your position.' Because when a person sees what objections are presented to him, he has to reinforce his arguments and then his words come out well clarified." (Mordechai Y. Leiner, *Mei HaShiloach* Vol. 1 [Bnei Brak: Mishor Publishing, 2007], 15, in his commentary on Genesis 2:18, *E'esseh lo ezer kenegdo*).

13   The clarifications provided in parentheses are either mine or are borrowed from the Steinsaltz translation. In both cases, these additions are designed to clarify the meaning of the text.

14   The expression "his statements were sharply formulated" refers to the sage's breadth of knowledge of Jewish inherited legal traditions.

each statement made by Rabbi Yochanan, Rabbi Elazar would say to him, "There is a *baraita* [a textual source serving as legal precedent] supporting your position." But Rabbi Yochanan was not comforted by Rabbi Elazar's remarks and he said to him, "Do you suppose that you are like Rabbi Shimon the son of Lakish? Whenever I would say something, the son of Lakish would raise twenty-four objections to what I said and I would then give him twenty-four answers. And the subject would thereby be clarified [literal translation: 'and the learning is thereby expanded']. But all that you say to me is, 'There is a *baraita* that supports you.' Do you imagine I do not know that what I said is correct?"[15]

Rabbi Elazar is merely a *yes-man*, mobilizing textual support for Rabbi Yochanan's statements. This model is rejected as unsatisfactory. With Resh Lakish, both study partners seem to be active, with one partner challenging the other's statements. Moreover, this model displays the dynamics of objecting, questioning, and answering, and it focuses on the resulting clarification of the subject matter.

However, the time has come to reexamine the centuries-old admiration of the Rabbi Yochanan-Resh Lakish learning paradigm, taking into account the fact that Resh Lakish's death (and subsequently Rabbi Yochanan's as well) are attributed to an incident that purportedly stems from their conversational pattern. In addition, the remainder of the legend and some related sources shed a different light on Rabbi Yochanan's attitude toward Resh Lakish.

What Is the Ideal Learning Relationship?

This text uses its characters in an archetypical way to illustrate possible perceptions of learning partners' roles, exaggerating distinctive features of important rabbinical figures to the point of a comical or grotesque effect. Thus, the shift begins with a more critical reading of the passage and by considering two different perceptions of the roles that can be attributed to a co-learner: the yes-man and the sparring partner. Although it has been seen over the centuries as an endorsement of the latter relationship, this

---

15   Talmud, Tractate Baba Metzia 84a–84b.

legend can be read as a carefully crafted critique of both paradigms, favoring a third model that is found elsewhere in the Talmud. The narrative above describes Resh Lakish as active, but is he truly a free thinker, an equal in his interface with Rabbi Yochanan? Resh Lakish contributes to Rabbi Yochanan's understanding by challenging his arguments, but does Resh Lakish express independent opinions? In Rabbi Yochanan's retrospective description, Resh Lakish's understanding of the subject matter does not appear relevant or important within this purportedly two-sided learning. Rabbi Yochanan seems to see Resh Lakish as a sparring partner whose sole purpose is to improve the star player's performance, or sharpen his ideas. Is there intentional irony in Rabbi Yochanan's question to Rabbi Elazar, "Do you imagine I do not know that what I said is correct"? Rabbi Yochanan's actual and potential learning partners have value only as facilitators of his own understanding. Rabbi Yochanan is not seeking alternative or opposing views *per se*, but a sparring partner's directed objections that will strengthen his conviction regarding what he *already* knows. It may be that Resh Lakish also learns from the exchange of objections and answers. A sparring partner may gain understanding, but that is of little consequence to the main player, who does not feel a need to help increase his partner's knowledge or skills, or even take into account the possibility that he himself could gain new insights through a real, collaborative exchange of ideas.

The full story of the legend begins with a description of Rabbi Yochanan's first encounter with Resh Lakish. Rabbi Yochanan is bathing in the Jordan River. The knowledgeable reader already knows that Rabbi Yochanan is handsome and clean-shaven, while Resh Lakish is a former gladiator or the leader of a band of bandits—in short, a man of great physical strength:[16]

> One day Rabbi Yochanan was swimming in the Jordan River. Resh Lakish saw him [according to several manuscripts the text renders here: "and believed him to be a woman. He plunged his spear into the ground"][17] and jumped into the Jordan after him.

---

[16]   Ibid.

[17]   Boyarin, *Carnal Israel*, 216.

Rabbi Yochanan said to him, "Your strength should be directed to
the study of Torah." Resh Lakish said to him, "Your beauty should
be directed to women." Rabbi Yochanan answered, "If you repent
I will give you my sister in marriage; she is more beautiful than
I am." Resh Lakish undertook to repent. He wished to climb back
to the riverbank to get his clothing but was unable to do so.

Why does Resh Lakish jump into the water? If he is a robber,
perhaps he means to harm Rabbi Yochanan and steal his belongings.
It also is possible that Resh Lakish is driven by sexual attraction,
suggested by the phallic symbol of the spear.[18] Regardless of Resh
Lakish's exact motive, the legend presents an encounter between
two very different human beings. Resh Lakish is driven by powerful
sexual/instinctual urges; Rabbi Yochanan is driven by intellectual
and spiritual motives, which are dedicated to the study of Torah.
Rabbi Yochanan invites Resh Lakish to channel his physical
strength in the service—that is, the study and the practice—of
Torah. To induce him to make this change, Rabbi Yochanan offers
his own sister—a puzzling and unsettling proposition, as consent
is indispensable for a marriage according to Talmudic law. Resh
Lakish seems ready to undergo a radical change. He dedicates
himself to the study of Torah as well as to a totally new social
environment where physical strength is not the most valued asset.
The reader does not know whether he has been searching for an
opportunity such as Rabbi Yochanan's offer, due to Talmudic
legends' typically minimal description of emotions and inner
thoughts, which must be inferred from actions and events. In this
case, the symbolic nature of the setting may be telling: natural water
serves in Judaism and elsewhere as a symbol of a new life that
grows in the maternal womb. The metaphor of Resh Lakish's
inability to climb up onto the riverbank could reflect his deep
existential expectation and readiness for transformation. He
immediately becomes devoid of the physical strength that had
been his defining characteristic. Furthermore, Resh Lakish is unable

---

[18]   Ibid. Also, in the second century, beards served as a central distinctive feature
between sexes, so the beardless Rabbi Yochanan may have appeared to be
a woman from afar.

to grasp his clothes, which literarily represent social identity. The simple act of emerging from a river comprises Resh Lakish's transformative moment. He cannot put his clothes back on, because he does not want to be, or perhaps he no longer is, the same person. He is reaching for a new environment and a very different cultural system—the culture of the Talmudic academy:

> Rabbi Yochanan personally tutored Resh Lakish; he taught him Bible and Mishna[19] and made him into a great scholar.

Rabbi Yochanan takes Resh Lakish under his wing. The unequal dynamic is natural at this stage. Rabbi Yochanan is the one who teaches, while Resh Lakish is the one who absorbs, learns, and receives the knowledge. The syntax of this sentence presents Rabbi Yochanan three times as the active subject and Resh Lakish as the passive object of Rabbi Yochanan's actions: *tutored, taught, made*. The next passage describes an incident that occurs later, when Resh Lakish has been recognized as a great scholar and serves as Rabbi Yochanan's study partner:

> One day there was a difference of opinion in the study hall [of the Talmudic academy]: A sword and a knife and a dagger and a spear and a handsaw and a sickle—from when are they susceptible to ritual impurity? From the time that their manufacture is complete. And from when is their manufacture complete? Rabbi Yochanan says, "From when he tempers them in the furnace."

The sages* are trying to distinguish the status of a collection of components, which are not susceptible to ritual impurity, from an end product, which Jewish law regards as susceptible.[20] Among

---

19   The *Mishna* is the first major written redaction of the Jewish oral tradition. It is also the first major work of Rabbinic Judaism and serves as the text at the center of the sages' debate in the Talmud. It was redacted around 220 CE by Rabbi Yehudah Hanassi but includes legal views of rabbinic sages known as the *Tanna'im*, "reciters," who were also entrusted with memorizing and passing down traditions from the first century BCE.

20   According to Jewish law, an object can become ritually impure in a number of ways, for example, through contact with a dead human body, certain dead animals including most insects and all lizards (see *Leviticus*, 11:29–32), and certain bodily fluids. An object that is ritually impure is thereby rendered unsuitable

the objects discussed are a knife, a sword, and a dagger. Rabbi Yochanan says that once these objects are tempered in the furnace, they acquire their full status. At this point, according to their usual dynamic, Resh Lakish should pose a series of twenty-four objections based on the internal logic of the existing system of law, of which Rabbi Yochanan is a master. Yet:

> Resh Lakish said, "From when he furbishes them in water."

Resh Lakish's intervention here is different, and thus he is violating Rabbi Yochanan's expectations of him as a sparring partner. From a literary perspective, limiting the context of this episodic storyline, this is the first time that Resh Lakish explicitly contradicts Rabbi Yochanan by interjecting his *own* opinion, presumably based on his experience before entering the Talmudic academy.

Rabbi Yochanan Strikes Back

Rabbi Yochanan's reaction is staggering:

> Rabbi Yochanan said to him, "A robber understands about robbery."

Rabbi Yochanan is facing, apparently for the first time, a situation in which Resh Lakish voices knowledge that may exceed his own. Rabbi Yochanan does not say "a *former* robber," much less express appreciation of Resh Lakish's input. Rabbi Yochanan's response—an *ad hominem* argument—is to avoid intellectual debate by reducing Resh Lakish to his former identity. Rabbi Yochanan's cutting statement is particularly insulting because, as the reader knows, Resh Lakish has undergone a profound existential change. Moreover, the jab is off-topic, shifting to the practice of robbery itself, as opposed to the potential tools of that trade.[21]

---

for certain uses until it undergoes predefined purification actions. An object's components are not susceptible to ritual impurity; only fully manufactured objects are.

21 Note the symbolic connection between the water mentioned here, in reference to the manufacturing process, and Resh Lakish's crucial moment of identity

Rabbi Yochanan is sure that what he says "is correct," so there is no point in having the learning partner introduce another view. From his perspective, Resh Lakish is transgressing an unspoken agreement, and his reaction is merciless. He seeks to undermine Resh Lakish's moral right to take on this new role in the learning relationship by reminding him of his deplorable origins, which provided him with this particular knowledge. This section brutally reinforces Rabbi Yochanan's image as a self-centered, domineering character and raises the issue of power relationships in the dynamics of teaching and learning. This image is further reinforced in subsequent sections. But first, the text describes Resh Lakish's reaction:

> Resh Lakish said to him, "And what good have you done me? There they called me 'master' and here they call me 'master.'"

Resh Lakish's reply is puzzling at first glance. How does it address Rabbi Yochanan's *ad hominem* criticism? What is Resh Lakish trying to say? Resh Lakish takes both the content and the timing of Rabbi Yochanan's attempt to silence him as symptomatic of the way he runs matters in the Talmudic academy. Essentially, he says, in spite of the notable differences in values and norms between this environment and my old society of robbers, human relationships remain the same. In my former life, I was the leader or the "master," with physical strength giving me power. When I joined the society of Torah study and began learning in the study hall, I expected to enter a culture in which relationships were governed by human dialogue in the common pursuit of knowledge and understanding, not authoritarian dynamics; but I was wrong, for here, too, I am called "master"—here, too, there is a hierarchy of power.

---

change, which took place in the water as well. Resh Lakish holds the view that the manufactured object is completed when it is furbished in the water. This may refer to his encounter with Rabbi Yochanan in the water. He may be asserting that he should then already have been treated as a full member of society, even though he had much to learn.

True, Resh Lakish is saying, this society is centered on Torah learning, but if I am still demeaned as a robber when I attempt to voice my opinion or share my knowledge in the study hall, then clearly power and competition continue to determine human relationships, rather than the recognition of my value as an individual with independent ideas.[22] Here, too, they call me "master," this time based on my intellectual capacity and my position as *your* student and as *your* learning partner. Status here in the Talmudic academy is not truly different from status among robbers or gladiators.[23] My title and my social status are solely the result of the roles that you, Rabbi Yochanan, through your power, have assigned the members of the Talmudic academy. I now realize that the societal structure in this study hall is in fact similar to the robbers' company: both are founded on power and control.

So, he concludes, what do you think you have contributed to my life? Have you just deceived me, convincing me that I was entering a culture with fundamentally different values at the heart of relationships and of learning interactions in particular?

The Fatal Spiritual Blow

Rabbi Yochanan said to him, "I have done you good by bringing you under the wings of the *Shechina** [the divine presence]. Rabbi Yochanan was deeply offended and Resh Lakish became ill.

Rabbi Yochanan's answer is so devastating to Resh Lakish that it sickens him. Unable to respond to Rabbi Yochanan's last statement, Resh Lakish is rendered at least literarily, speechless from this point onward. His voice is no longer heard in the text. In silence, he succumbs to illness and death. What in Rabbi Yochanan's answer is so devastating that it leads to Resh Lakish's death? Is it that Rabbi Yochanan is ignoring his student and study partner's valuable argument, or is Rabbi Yochanan actually addressing Resh Lakish's remarks?

---

[22] Kosman, *Massekhet Gvarim*, 40–41.

[23] Ibid.

Resh Lakish Speaks Again: The Third Paradigm

While Resh Lakish is never recorded as speaking again, his disciples express his views elsewhere:[24]

> Rabbi Yirmiyah said in the name of Rabbi Shimon the son of Lakish: "When two scholars are amiable to each other in their discussion of halacha, the Holy One, blessed be He, gives heed to them" . . . Rabbi Abba said in the name of Rabbi Shimon the son of Lakish: "When two scholars pay heed to each other in halacha, the Holy One, blessed be He, listens to their voice . . . But if they do not do thus, they cause the *Shechina* to depart from Israel."[25]

These statements shed light on the confrontation in our legend. In both statements, Resh Lakish indicates the kind of learning relationship he is longing for, quite far from his confined role as a sparring partner. He stresses the synergy, the exchange of ideas between individuals who share the common purpose of learning from and through each other with forbearance and openness.

Rashi explains the expression "two scholars are amiable to each other" as a calm exchange of ideas, so that the scholars can learn from each other. He interprets the expression "when two scholars pay heed to each other" as "teach one another and understand from each other." In contrast to the roles of yes-man and sparring partner, Resh Lakish is suggesting that paired study not be used exclusively for the sake of one's own learning but serve as a reflective and genuine dialogue, in spirit and in deed. In this third paradigm, the partners' learning is interdependent and intertwined, and—most importantly—they see themselves as assuming responsibility for one another's learning.[26] This requires attention, openness, and

---

24   Rubenstein, *Talmudic Stories*, discusses the interconnectedness of Talmudic legends.

25   Talmud, Tractate Shabbat 63a.

26   This is also how this text has been interpreted by Rabbi Isaiah Horovitz (1565–1630), known as the *Shelah Hakadosh* after the title of his book. Isaiah Horowitz, *The Two Tablets of the Covenant* (Amsterdam: n.p., 1697), 66a: "That their argumentative learning will be performed in a calm way, not by shouting. And each one will make sure to understand his partner thoroughly, and then he will admit the truth." He continues by interpreting the text to include reciprocal

genuine caring. This added element of responsibility infuses the learning dynamic with a fundamental ethical dimension to which an individual becomes committed.

God and Relationships

The metaphor of God's listening is used in both statements attributed to Resh Lakish. They twice note that God ("the Holy One, blessed be He") pays attention to the dialogical relationship between learning partners, and that when joint study does not include this kind of listening to one's partner, "they cause the *Shechina* to depart from Israel." The metaphors of God's listening and the presence of the *Shechina* suggest an intrinsic connection between God's participation and the actual dialogical relationship, especially if "God" is understood primarily as some transcendent quality of a genuine interpersonal experience. In fact, "*Shechina*" is a name used for God that indicates God's immanent presence in the world, and particularly in human relationships.[27] From this

---

support of interpretation even in the case of disagreement: "The learner will bring support to his partner's understanding if the latter runs into a difficulty according to his own interpretation. The learner will then help his partner to solve the difficulty, as we often find in the Talmud (e.g., Talmud, Tractate Baba Metzia 22a): 'Abaye explained the problem according to Rava, etc.,' despite his disagreement." See Holzer with Kent, *A Philosophy of Havruta*, 124–125; 172–183, for a discussion of the challenge of cultivating such a supportive approach in the midst of disagreement. Emmanuel Levinas holds a radical view on the relationship between "responsibility" and "responding," where the former is always a given, whether or not there is any reciprocity. See the following account of Levinas: "For Levinas, the Other comes from up high— the Other is teacher before partner. There is no symmetry in being responsible, that is, in being answerable and addressable. Since responsibility as response-ability is the very beginning of subjectivity, I am always already answerable to the Other's call, always already approachable, open, predisposed toward the Other" (Amit Pinchevski, *By Way of Interruption: Levinas and the Ethics of Communication* [Pittsburgh: Duquesne University Press, 2005], 75). For the connection between ethics and transcendence in my overall discussion on attuned learning, see Chapter One, Footnote 25 and Chapter Eight, Footnote 12.

27   Efraim Elimelech Urbach, *Chazal: Emunot VeDeot* (Jerusalem: Magnes Press, Hebrew University, 1979), 43, 48.

perspective, transcendence is not surpassing the range of human experience but, on the contrary, concerns what lies *within* the human experience. Pointing to God's presence is less a claim of the presence of a metaphysical being, who rules by reward and punishment, as it is of a quality of the encounter between two learners. It refers to the learner's experience of opening up and coming knowingly to see, think, and feel differently due to a genuine interaction with the learning partner.

This insight from Tractate Shabbat uncovers the cause of Resh Lakish's deep distress in the legend. Rabbi Yochanan says, "I have done you good by bringing you under the wings of the *Shechina*." For Rabbi Yochanan, the sacred dimension resides "under the wings of the *Shechina*" — a static location, perhaps the physical space under the roof of the holy hall of study or even under the metaphorical canopy of Torah knowledge. The divine presence does not, however, impose any ethical claim on the individual in the learning interaction. In contrast, for Resh Lakish, the sacred dimension resides within human experience in the very modes of interaction of two people who open themselves up to each other and take responsibility for each other's learning.

Resh Lakish's extreme reaction to Rabbi Yochanan's claim, "I have done you good by bringing you under the wings of the *Shechina*," is now understandable. As he listens to Rabbi Yochanan's conceptualization of the divine presence, Resh Lakish realizes that their conflict concerning his role, and the kind of silence that Rabbi Yochanan has tried to impose on him, reflect not only a disagreement regarding power and authoritarian relationships but one that is also deeply rooted in fundamentally different religious outlooks. Rabbi Yochanan takes for granted that the divine presence resides in the hall of study, since this is where Torah is studied. In contrast, Resh Lakish's quest, and his expectation, was to find a social environment where the divine presence is perceived as finding residence in the very heart of learning relationships.[28] This

---

28   Emmanuel Levinas, writes: "God's reign depends on me. God has subordinated his efficacy — his association with the real and the very presence of the real — to my merit or demerit and so God reigns only by the intermediary of an ethical

radical realization is devastating, as it undermines all of Resh Lakish's hopes and longings—and his efforts—from the time he set out to make his extreme existential and societal change. Now, and for the rest of the literary structure of the story, he becomes silent. In the face of Rabbi Yochanan's rebuke, Resh Lakish feels that he has not only lost his voice as a learner, but he also has lost his inner, religious voice in the study hall. This leads him to a deep emotional-spiritual crisis and closes him off to further human interaction, right up to the time of his own death.

Harsh Caricature

The text presents a powerful critique of egocentric learning and emphasizes the necessity of an ethical dimension of learning. To reach that end, the legend takes the bold, self-centered image of Rabbi Yochanan to its extreme, in spite of his status as a leading Talmudic sage:

> Rabbi Yochanan's sister came to him and wept. She said to him: "Act for the sake of my children." He said to her, "Leave your orphans to me, I will preserve them alive (Jeremiah 49:11)." She said, "Act for the sake of my widowhood." Rabbi Yochanan answered, "And let your widows trust in me (ibid)."

Rabbi Yochanan's sister fears the worst. Her husband, Resh Lakish, is deeply depressed. She asks her brother to take the first step toward reconciliation so that Resh Lakish may recover. Rabbi Yochanan says he will instead care for his orphaned nieces and nephews and for his widowed sister after Resh Lakish's death. His coldness is stunning. The full meaning of Rabbi Yochanan's

---

order, an order in which one being is answerable for another [. . .] The human is the possibility of a being-for-the-other. That possibility is the justification of all existing. The world is justified in its being by human dis-interestment, which concretely signifies consent to the Torah, *and therefore surely already studies of Torah*. More important than God's omnipotence is the subordination of that power to man's ethical consent" (Emmanuel Levinas, "Judaism and Kenosis," *In the Time of the Nations* [New York: Continuum, 2007], 112–113, my emphasis).

answers, however, is embedded in the biblical verse that he quotes: "Leave your orphans to me, I will preserve them alive; and let your widows trust in me."

Admiel Kosman notes a subtle literary device the narrator uses to provide an important insight.[29] Who is the subject of the cited verse, who cares for widows and orphans? None other than God! Thus, through the use of a biblical source, the text offers an even more shocking portrayal of Rabbi Yochanan as so self-aggrandizing that he compares himself to God. With this caricature in mind, the reader can see how various details of the legend foreshadow this understated message. Rabbi Yochanan views himself as having "made" Resh Lakish: he personally tutored him, taught him, and brought him under the wings of the divine presence. Rabbi Yochanan prefers that learning partners be confined to the role of sparring partners—serving only his learning needs, without regard for their own. This characterization also explains the ease with which Rabbi Yochanan pledges his sister to Resh Lakish without consulting her.[30] Every detail of the legend implies his sense of power, his decisions, and his ability to control circumstances and individuals—certainly not qualities that are conducive to a dialogical orientation in joint learning.[31]

---

[29]   Kosman, *Massechet Gvarim*, 44.

[30]   In addition, a symbolic gender-oriented reading is in place. As already noticed by Boyarin, in *Carnal Israel*, "He plunged his spear into the ground" clearly indicates a phallic symbol, which generates an association of conquest and domination as a portrayal of Resh Lakish's original way of being in the world. But a reversal of attitudes occurs in the story, as it is Rabbi Yochanan who disposes of people and seeks to dominate them, not being able to engage in a (symbolically) feminine, receptive way of being, exemplified in his attitudes toward his sister. I thank Yehoshua Feffer for bringing my attention to this connection.

[31]   Iser, *The Act of Reading*, 180–181, writes that when literary characters seem to project a complete representation, one can focus on the "selective decisions that must be taken if the character is to be presented in such a way that we are able to identify him. In this case we are concerned not with the illusion of reality but with the patterns of external reality from which the selection of elements has been made [. . .] [E]ven if the character is presented in such a way that it simulates reality, this is not an end in itself but a sign for a broader meaning."

It is this image of Rabbi Yochanan's extreme self-centeredness that leads to the section of the legend that is most cited among scholars in idealizing the Rabbi Yochanan-Resh Lakish partnership, as discussed above.

The narrative continues:

> Rabbi Yochanan began rending his clothes and weeping and said, "Where are you, son of Lakish? Where are you, son of Lakish?" And he cried out until his mind slipped from him. The sages pleaded for mercy on his behalf and he died.

The end of the legend is tragic, and not just because both characters die. Rabbi Yochanan seems to have some remorse regarding his previous beliefs and choices. He rends his clothes (a traditional mourning ritual at the death of close relatives), reminiscent of the opening scene in which Resh Lakish cannot grasp his former clothes. The legend does not say what has brought Rabbi Yochanan to his realization; perhaps the emptiness has made him recognize Resh Lakish's value as an individual and has led him to realize that his previous view—regarding Resh Lakish only as a sparring partner— was so drastically mistaken that it could lead to death. Along the literal death within the narrative this may also be a metaphorical death of the learning relationship, when it completely loses its ethical-spiritual character. Through the symbolism of rending his clothes, Rabbi Yochanan seems to wish he had adopted another way of being in the world in general, and in his social role as a teacher and learning partner in particular. Even if Rabbi Yochanan's final words reflect a realization of the destructiveness of his existential choices, the story ends in tragedy. Whereas it began with two charismatic and life-filled characters, it concludes with death and desolation. Learning only happens through partnership. When one member of the dyad dies, the second must die.[32] This disastrous closure allows the reader no escape from the ideas reflected in this story; there is no redemption. The reader faces the weightiness and the tremendous implications of how one perceives the role of the partner in the learning dynamic.

---

[32]   I owe this insight to Marc Brettler.

Attuned Learning: Contemporary Resonances

Never before has dialogical learning attracted as much interest as it has in the past few decades.[33] Burgeoning psychological theories contain new conceptualizations of the social nature of learning.[34] Philosophers, too, have been addressing its interpersonal dimension by focusing on the role of human dialogue. They stress its moral quality, with its basis in mutual respect and egalitarianism, as well as the epistemological advantages of dialogue as a means of acquiring knowledge.[35] And educational researchers have been expanding the use of various forms of conversational learning at an unprecedented rate.[36] Robert N. Bellah points out the dangers

---

[33] See Roy Baumeister, "How the Self Became a Problem: A Psychological Review of Historical Research," *Journal of Personality and Social Psychology* 52, no. 1 (1987): 163–176, for a discussion that the idea of "self" developed in Western cultures from the early modern age. Martin Buber begins his chronological review of the history of the dialogical principle with authors of the eighteenth century in Buber, *Between Man and Man*.

[34] Lev S. Vygotsky, *Mind in Society, the Development of Higher Psychological Processes* (Cambridge: Harvard University Press, 1978); Barbara Rogoff, *Apprenticeship in Thinking: Cognitive Development in Social Context* (New York: Oxford University Press, 1990).

[35] Martin Buber, *I and Thou* (New York: Charles Scribner's Sons, 1970); Nicholas Burbules and Bertram C. Bruce, "Theory and Research on Teaching as Dialogue," in *Handbook of Research on Teaching 4th Edition*, ed. Virginia Richardson (Washington, DC: American Educational Research Association, 2001), 1102–1121; Freire, *The Pedagogy of the Oppressed*; Paulo Freire, *The Politics of Education* (South Hadley: Bergin and Garvey, 1985). See also Holzer with Kent, *A Philosophy of Havruta*, 167–207, for my own work on paired learning.

[36] For a discussion about the power of transforming classroom education from lecture to dialogue, see Roland C. Christensen et al., *Education for Judgment: The Artistry of Discussion Leadership*, ed. Roland C. Christensen, David A. Garvin, and Ann Sweet (Cambridge, MA: Harvard Business School, 1991). Also Faith Gabelnick et al.'s report on the power of collaborative groups and learning communities: Faith Gabelnick et al., *Learning Communities: Creating Connections Among Students, Faculty, and Disciplines*, ed. Faith Gabelnick, John MacGregor, Roberta S. Matthews, and Barabra Leigh Smith (San Francisco: Jossey-Bass, 1990). Sophie Haroutunian-Gordon provides an example of a pedagogical implementation in *Turning the Soul: Teaching through Conversation in the High School* (Chicago: University of Chicago Press, 1991) and *Learning to Teach Through Discussion: The Art of Turning the Soul* (New Haven: Yale University Press, 2009).

of individuals' belief in a singular self at the cost of interpersonal relationships and trust.[37] In an educational climate that fosters a narrow view of individual growth as its highest value, a student may be ill-prepared to develop character traits such as caring about the learning of others. According to Charles Derber, certain unconscious patterns of conversational narcissism reflect habitual self-absorption that is unselfconsciously expressed in conversation patterns.[38]

On this backdrop, the rabbinic texts discussed in this chapter create a provocative and brutally frank paradigm of self-involvement in learning, and promote identification with Resh Lakish, champion of an empathic view of collaborative learning. More specifically, these texts prompt contemporary educators to consider four aspects of attuned learning as they conceptualize the profile of collaborative learners.

The first aspect pertains to what it means to grow as a co-learner, and implies that collaborative learning is not merely an instrument for the improvement of the learner's comprehension of the subject matter. Beyond the oppositional or harmonious character of the learning interaction, attuned collaborative learning presumes sincere concern for the joint project of sense-making. While this idea is reflected in the texts discussed in Chapter Three, the legend additionally addresses the learner's need to care about, empathize with, and assist another person in her own learning process. Alienation is a key factor in educational failure, as summarized by education scholars Charles Bingham and Alexander M. Sidorkin who point out teachers' low expectations, the breakdown of social order, and academic failure as reflecting "only symptoms of the much deeper problem of alienation."[39] Despite the importance attached

---

[37] Bellah, *Habits of the Heart*; Robert N. Bellah, Richard Madsen, William M. Sullivan, Ann Swidler, and Steven M. Tipton, *The Good Society* (New York: Vintage Books, 1991).

[38] Charles Derber, *The Pursuit of Attention: Power and Individualism in Everyday Life* (Oxford: Oxford University Press, 2000), 25–26.

[39] Charles Bingham and Alexander M. Sidorkin, *No Education without Relation* (New York: Peter Lang, 2004), 6. In the words of Anita Vangelisti et al., there is

to classroom discussion in modern educational settings, students often are habituated to follow the external rules of conversation—such as not interrupting each other—but are not accustomed to cultivating a more intersubjective relationship. To use the terminology of Zygmunt Bauman, students' relationships during classes are limited to a type of conventional *being with*.[40] In contrast, these rabbinic texts underscore a mode of being together that is a *being for*, an attunement that is *to the benefit of* the learning partner's growth.[41] This spirit of true engagement among learning partners attempts to transcend the self-involvement commonly found in "collaborative" learning. When one learner understands another's learning as being within the scope of his or her own responsibility, and when this deep concern translates into concrete solicitousness and effective assistance, the student can be said to embody

---

a "pattern rooted in American culture that supports a form of individualism that, in turn, encourages self-interest" (Anita L. Vangelisti, Mark L., Knapp, and John A. Daly, "Conversational Narcissism," *Communication Monographs* 57 [1990]: 251). This manifests itself in four ways: as self-importance and self-absorption that are experienced by others as arrogance and that deny others' needs; as an exploitation of others; as expressions of exhibitionism that make one the constant center of attention; and as an impersonal relationship that does not protect the other's privacy.

40   Zygmunt Bauman, *Life in Fragments: Essays in Postmodern Morality* (Oxford: Blackwell Publishers, 1995), 51–52.

41   Psychologist Carl Rogers attempts to conceptualize what he learned to be central to healthy and effective interpersonal relationships in the helping professions (psychotherapist, religious worker, guidance counselor, social worker, clinical psychologist), and in facilitating learning in particular. He indicates three fundamental qualities or attitudes that are particularly important in facilitating learning: congruence, acceptance, and empathic understanding. Rogers talks about these with regard to the teacher as qualities that contribute to a climate of self-initiated experiential learning. The need to impress others, often by trying to present oneself as knowledgeable, is common in formal learning environments and may thus also characterize collaborative learning. Rogers' insistence on congruence refers to the individual's effort to reduce the façade that he wears in a relationship. Empathic understanding refers to the ability of learners to understand each other's reactions and to have a good sense of the way learning occurs by their peers. See Carl R. Rogers, "The Interpersonal Relationship: The Core of Guidance," in *Person to Person: The Problem of Being Human, a New Trend in Psychology*, ed. Carl Rogers et al. (Lafayette: Real People Press, 1967), 85–101.

a "Resh Lakish" attitude—a far cry from Derber's conversational narcissism.

A second aspect of attuned learning is conveyed by the depiction of Rabbi Yochanan as a self-centered scholar, which makes a strong claim: achieving scholarship and greatness in Torah knowledge, as Rabbi Yochanan has, does not guarantee the cultivation of spiritual-ethical excellence, at least in the context of learning relationships. This suggests a need for revising and broadening the scope of the curriculum to include pedagogical engagement with attuned learning in and through students' learning activities and experiences.

A third aspect is the connection between an individual's basic attitude toward a study partner and her central dispositions and core personality traits. Resh Lakish's yearning makes the reader aware of an ethical dimension, of which taking responsibility for each other's learning is a defining criterion. The legend suggests that when learning with another person is only self-serving, narcissistic and controlling attitudes in other social relationships may go unchecked—such as Rabbi Yochanan's disregard for his sister's feelings. No amount of formal knowledge, no official leadership status, nor any sacredness of the content of Torah can exempt an individual from the ethical demands of attuned learning. Educators must consider the reciprocal connections between students' ways of being and operating in learning relationships as well as their attitudes and behavior in general life interactions, challenging prevailing educational approaches that operate on a radical separation between academic achievement and moral development.

A fourth, subtle aspect of attuned learning is the elusive nature of the commitment to care actively for a partner's learning. It cannot be encapsulated by a prescribed list of behaviors, codes, or precepts; the process is not completely cognitive. It requires the cultivation of empathy on the part of not only the teacher but also any co-learner, echoing Rodgers' and Raider-Roth's concept of *presence* discussed in Chapter One.[42] Resh Lakish's personal journey and his yearning for empathy as expressed in Tractate Shabbat show

---

42   Rodgers and Raider-Roth, "Presence in Teaching."

that this commitment is not a matter of a conceptual or theoretical engagement existing prior to the relationship, but ideally one that grows through the contextual, concrete, and personal connections people develop in the very nexus of learning. Educational thinking about various tenets of attuned learning will by necessity expand beyond the more rules-based and technical boundaries of curriculum discourse.

***

Maimonides wrote that "the gates of interpretation are not sealed."[43] Subtle literary arrangements, as in this legend, have elicited new interpretations in recent years. Different interpretive lenses generate additional insights, and reading this text through the lens of attuned learning has contributed to its understanding. At the same time, it is worth turning the lens around and considering collaborative learning from the vantage point of rabbinic literature's central concerns such as rabbinic authority, authentic legal ruling, and the tension between transmission of tradition versus the possibility of human innovation.[44]

It is from this perspective that Avi Sagi points out another alternative interpretation of this legend that contributes insight regarding collaborative learning. The "Sinai" scholar is concerned with the study and transmission of tradition as it has been inherited, while the "uprooting mountains" scholar is inclined to seek new or hidden meanings through logical inference and interpretation. The former is eager to hold onto an original legal-religious "truth," while the latter understands the legal-halachic *system* as also possessing contingent legal-religious "truth." In his book, Sagi shows how different variations of these tensions have played out in rabbinic literature.[45] The Talmud itself describes Resh Lakish as a sage who

---

43   Maimonides, *Guide for the Perplexed* (New York: Cosimo Classics, 2007), 199.

44   See the introduction to Part Two and my reference to Sagi, *The Open Canon*. See also Avi Sagi, *Ne-emanut Hilchatit: Ben Petichut Lesgirut* (Ramat Gan: Bar Ilan University Press, 2012), 91–115.

45   Ibid.

"uproots mountains," with Rabbi Yochanan as a "Sinai" type.[46] As someone who embodies the Sinai orientation, Rabbi Yochanan sees the role of collaborative learning as a way both to master and sharpen the understanding of the inherited tradition. To that end, he uses a learning partner who responds to him with questions that help him sharpen, and thereby broaden, his own understanding. By simply supporting Rabbi Yochanan's statements, Rabbi Elazar does not fulfill that role and is therefore dismissed. In contrast, by posing his twenty-four questions to Rabbi Yochanan's statements, Resh Lakish helps sharpen the inherited tradition. The crisis occurs when Resh Lakish exhibits a characteristic of a sage who "uproots mountains," for whom studying Torah involves bringing in one's outside experience in the quest for new truths that may not yet have been articulated. For a Sinai scholar, this move breaches a basic tenet of Torah study. In his reply, "a robber understands about robbery," Rabbi Yochanan is reminding Resh Lakish that the origin of his expertise lies outside the tradition and is thus not welcome in the hall of study. In his response, Resh Lakish essentially says, "If this is the case, I now realize that as societies, the bandits' circle and the hall of study are fairly identical. In both there are well-defined rules, and nothing external is allowed to challenge them." Rabbi Yochanan answers, "I have brought you under the wings of the *Shechina*." In other words, "You are missing the point of being part of this society. It is to reside under the canopy of the *inherited* tradition."

This interpretation situates the legend as a foundational story within rabbinic literature, because it addresses one of this tradition's central issues: the tension between inherited tradition and the possibility of its creative renewal by the power of human thought and knowledge. There is a clear difference in the main foci of each of these alternative interpretations. Sagi's interpretation raises the question of the legitimate boundaries of the sources of halachic discourse, and expresses its concerns about the inviolable integrity of the halachic tradition. The interpretation offered earlier

---

[46]   Talmud, Tractate Sanhedrin 21a; Talmud, Tractate Sanhedrin 24a; as well as Rashi's commentary.

in the chapter brings to light this text's concern regarding the learner's perceptions and ways of interacting with a co-learner. Placing these two different interpretations side by side highlights that those who study Torah are inherently dedicated to certain beliefs and commitments. Those ideals should translate into caring not only about the subject matter and the tradition, but also about other human beings—their study partners. In this regard, a similar rabbinic text sharpens the disparity between the ways Resh Lakish and Rabbi Yochanan view collaborative learning, and reinforces the arrogance that the legend ascribes to Rabbi Yochanan. An allegorical interpretation of Exodus 31:18, which says that God was speaking *with* rather than *to* Moses before the giving of the second set of Tablets of the Law, explains:

> Rabbi Shimon the son of Lakish asked: What is the meaning of the phrase "of speaking with him"? It can be compared to a disciple whose master taught him Torah; before the pupil had learned it, the teacher would recite and he would repeat, but after he had acquired the knowledge, the teacher said to him: "Come, we will both recite." Similarly, when Moses went up to heaven, he began to recite the Torah after his Creator, but after he had learned it, God said: "Let us say it together"—hence the words "of speaking with him."

The content here is *recitation* of law, reflecting the central role of memorization in Talmudic culture, but also reminiscent of Rabbi Yochanan's Sinai orientation.[47] And yet, the emphasis is on the teacher's awareness of the change in the learning relationship, and his initiative in inviting the student into a shared, common learning activity that has an element of equality. Resh Lakish recognizes the difference in status between the teacher, who possesses the knowledge initially, and the student, whose role is to absorb the transmitted knowledge, but he highlights the subsequent collaborative aspect of the learning relationship. These lines echo his relationship with Rabbi Yochanan, which similarly started with a traditional teacher-student formula, and reflect Resh

---

[47] Martin S. Jaffee, *Torah in the Mouth: Writing and Oral Tradition in Palestinian Judaism 200 BCE–400 CE* (New York: Oxford University Press, 2001).

Lakish's later aspirations for a collaborative and dialogical learning relationship.

This midrash enhances the primary reading of the legend. It is sensitive to evolving and changing roles in teaching and learning. It underscores the need for both the recognition of the teacher's initial "master" status and her responsibilities, and the moral necessity for the teacher to create, over time, more space for the student's growth into a learning partner. Here, too, Resh Lakish is sharing an insight into his view of learning dynamics. Invoking nothing less than a parallel of God as teacher and Moses as disciple, Resh Lakish expresses what he believes it means to *speak with* someone. The effect is prescriptive: if God—who is omniscient and has nothing to gain by involving a human being in a dialogue—acts this way, then how much more necessary must it be for human beings to adopt this attitude? The juxtaposition of the legend with this text is striking and even ironic: Rabbi Yochanan, who has likened himself to God, eschews this opportunity to emulate God in his interactions with Resh Lakish.

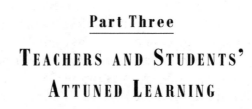

Part Three

TEACHERS AND STUDENTS' ATTUNED LEARNING

Introduction

TEACHING IN RABBINIC LITERATURE

> The study of Torah is more important than the
> rebuilding of the Temple.
>
> —*Babylonian Talmud, Tractate Megillah 16b*

Formal Aspects of "Talmud Torah"*

Rabbinic Judaism, which emerged in the first and second centuries
CE as a result of the Jews' exile and consequent decentralization,
places great emphasis on scholarship.[1] For two millennia, Jews have
studied the Torah* (the Five Books of Moses), the Talmud, and many
other religious texts. Torah study has practical purposes such as
knowledge of religious and legal laws and ritual service.[2] It is also
conceptualized as a practice worthy in and of itself, raised to the
status of God's worship, as in the expression "the study of Torah
for its own sake" (*Torah lishmah**).[3] Simon Rawidowicz discusses
a radical change in Jewish theology just before the destruction of the
Temple in 70 CE, as God begins to be portrayed as participating in
Torah study, a far cry from biblical military images. Thus, a midrash
imagines that one-third of God's time is spent studying Torah in the

---

[1] For a historical study on the establishment of rabbinic educational culture
from the second to the fourth centuries, see Hirschman, *The Stabilization of
Rabbinic Culture*.

[2] Assaf and Glick, *Mekorot Letoldot Hachinuch Hayehudi*.

[3] The Talmud debates which of the two is greater: study or action (practical
application of the Torah) and concludes that study is greater when it leads to
action (Talmud, Tractate Kiddushin 40b). For an extended discussion of *"Torah
lishmah"* in post-Talmudic rabbinic literature, see Lamm, *Torah Lishmah*.

*beit midrash** (the hall of study)[4] and God is described as a teacher and a *chavruta* learner[5] who studies the sages' interpretations.[6] Early rabbinic texts state that "the study of Torah prevails above all other commandments."[7] Torah study is obligatory for every man, notwithstanding social status or profession.[8] The term *talmud Torah* refers to the study and the teaching of Torah, and both activities are codified in religious law. From the Bible through the Jewish legal codes, parents are enjoined to teach the laws and the Exodus narrative to their children.[9] The parental obligation is expanded to include hiring a teacher, and communities are responsible for children's education as well.[10] The sages consider those who study

---

4   Talmud, Tractate Avodah Zarah 3b. God is also described as spending time teaching Torah to very young children. Simon Rawidowicz, *Iyounim BeMachshevet Israel* Vol. 1 (Jerusalem: Rubin Mass, 1969), 42. See also Stern, *Midrash and Theory*, 73–94.

5   Talmud, Tractate Brachot 63a; *Tractate Avodah Zarah*, 3b.

6   Talmud, Tractate Gittin 7a; Tractate Chagiga 15b.

7   Mishna Peah, 1: 1. The "other commandments" are listed in the same Mishna. Torah study as a fundamental characteristic of historical Judaism is a phenomenon that stands out in any broad view of cultures and religions. See for example Lamm, *Torah Lishmah* and Mordechai Breuer, *Ohale torah: Hayeshiva tavnita vetoldoteha* (Jerusalem: Merkaz Zalman Shazar Publication, 2004). Among quotes that prioritize the study of Torah, see for example: "Jerusalem was destroyed because the inhabitants neglected the teaching of their children" (Talmud, Tractate Sukkah 42a); "The world exists only by virtue of the breath coming from the mouths of school children engaged in their studies" (Talmud, Tractate Shabbat 119b); "Raba said, 'When man is led in for judgment he is asked, "Did you act with integrity, *did you fix times for learning*, did you engage in procreation, did you hope for salvation, did you engage in the dialectics of wisdom, did you understand one thing from another?"'" (Talmud, Tractate Shabbat 31a, my emphasis.)

8   Over the past several decades, women of various denominations within Judaism have appropriated traditional text-based learning as a central activity in their lives as well.

9   "And you shall teach it to your children," (Deuteronomy 6:7) and "And you shall tell your son on that day, saying: It is because of that which the Lord did for me when I came forth out of Egypt," (Exodus 13:8).

10   See Talmud, Tractate Baba Batra 21a.

in order to teach others particularly praiseworthy.[11] The centrality of *talmud Torah* reflects the centrality of cultural transmission in rabbinic culture. Tradition is perceived as proceeding from a foundational origin and destined to be renewed throughout the generations, turning the teaching of Torah into a vocation. Transmission passes along this heritage and the achievements of previous generations. Thus, *talmud Torah* involves the socialization of the individual into a set of beliefs, symbols, knowledge, practices, and rituals.[12] It is reflected in rabbinic literature's emphasis on repetition, memorization, and rote learning.[13] The primary aspect

---

11   *Ethics of the Fathers* 4: 5; Maimonides, *The Book of Commandments,* positive commandment 11: "We are commanded to study and to teach the wisdom of Torah. This is called Talmud Torah"; rabbinic texts emphasize the moral duty to teach: "Rabbi Yochanan further said, 'One who studies the Torah but does not teach it is like the myrtle in the wilderness whose fragrance is wasted'" (Talmud, Tractate Rosh Hashanah 23a). "Torah that is studied in order to teach is a 'Torah of lovingkindness,' but Torah that is not studied in order to teach is not a Torah of lovingkindness" (Talmud, Tractate Sukkah 49b). See also: "Anyone who withholds [the teaching of] a law from a student is as if he steals from the student's father's inheritance, as it says, '[. . .] it is an inheritance to the Congregation of Israel'" (Talmud, Tractate Sanhedrin 91b).

12   Socializing occurs in all social environments. Emile Durkheim (1858–1917) writes of modern societies: "Education is the influence exercised by adult generations on those that are not yet ready for social life. Its object is to arouse and to develop in the child a certain number of physical, intellectual and moral states which are demanded of him by both the political society as a whole and the special milieu for which he is specifically destined" (Emile Durkheim, *Education and Sociology* [New York: The Free Press, 1956], 71).

13   These aspects of learning are not limited to younger students or beginners. "Thus, for example, Resh Lakish made it his practice to repeat in systematic order his studies forty times corresponding to the forty days during which the Torah was given, and only then would he come before Rabbi Yochanan. Rabbi Adda the son of Abbahu made it his practice to repeat in systematic order his studies twenty-four times corresponding to the twenty-four books that embody the Torah, the Prophets, and the Hagiographa, and only then would he come before Raba" (Talmud, Tractate Ta'anit 8a). "He who repeats his studies a hundred times is not to be compared with him who repeats his studies a hundred and one times" (Talmud, Tractate Chagiga 9b). "Rabbi Yehoshua the son of Karcha said, 'Whoever studies the Torah and does not review it is likened unto one who sows without reaping'" (Talmud, Tractate Sanhedrin 99a). See also Hirshman, *The Stabilization of Rabbinic Culture,* 111–115.

of teaching is to assist and to prepare the student for receiving and identifying with the tradition, and it encompasses fashioning discipleship in the student. Thus, rabbinical tradition clearly favors the person who learns from a teacher over one who is self-taught.[14] It emphasizes the need for the learner to surpass herself, and it values the special efforts required to acquire Torah knowledge.[15] It is first the teacher who leads the student into such challenges, who assists her and provides her with opportunities to progress through her own efforts. The teacher of Torah teaches not only conceptual, intellectual, and practical knowledge; teaching Torah also entails the transmission of a *savoir-être*, a kind of knowing how to be in life, how to relate appropriately to others, to the environment, and to oneself. In a broad philosophical sense, what is taught is believed to contribute in some way to the student's growth as a human being, by advancing her understanding of the meaning of her existence.

"Experiential" Aspects of Talmud Torah

Beyond the formal concepts and impersonal structures of any educational tradition, the *experiential* aspects of teaching and learning, as reflected in rabbinic texts, are concrete, subjective, dynamic, and at times unpredictable. Rabbinic texts address the relationship between the study of the inherited tradition and the learner's personal feelings and ability to generate new insights in that tradition. The contribution of innovative ideas is through rational and intellectual reasoning (*sevara*)* in Talmudic discourse. Similarly, a wide range of interpretive strategies serve as venues for legal, ritual, and philosophical innovations, which are broadly conceived as expanding, deepening, and enriching—rather than altering—the tradition.[16] For example, "If you listen to the old,

---

14   Talmud, Tractate Brachot 63b: "One who engages in solitary study will be cursed, grow foolish, and ultimately fall into sin."

15   Talmud, Tractate Sanhedrin 42b, uses the term "the war of Torah study"; Talmud, Tractate Megillah 6a speaks about "exertion" as central to Torah study.

16   See Introduction to Part Two.

you will be able to listen to the new, but 'if your heart turn away' (Deuteronomy 30:17), you will no more listen."[17] Another text expresses a similar view: "One should always study the Torah first and meditate in it afterwards, as it is said, 'the Law of the Lord,' and then, 'And in his own law he meditates.'"[18]

The Talmud echoes people's personal preferences toward specific parts of the transmitted tradition and presents it as a guiding value for one's Torah study: "A man can learn well only that part of the Torah which is his heart's desire, for it is said, 'But whose delight is in the law of the Lord' (Psalms 1:2)."[19] But Rava, the great fourth-century CE Babylonian scholar who is the author of this teaching, clarifies that God's Torah has to be acquired first by study, and only then the Torah can become one's own. He also states that study should always precede reflective thinking.[20] Individual students develop and grow through the study of the inherited tradition and a sense of socialization into a historical continuity.

Teachers' subtle experiences reflect a similar outlook:

> Nachman the son of Rabbi Chisda gave the following exposition: "What is the meaning of the verse, 'Your ointments yield a sweet fragrance?' To what may a scholar be compared? To a bottle of fragrant oil. When it is opened, it gives off an aromatic scent, but when covered, its pleasant odor does not spread. Moreover, when a scholar teaches others, things that were hidden become revealed to him, as it is said, 'Therefore do the maidens (*alamot*) love thee,' which may be read to mean 'the hidden (*alumot*) love thee.'"[21]

The relationship between teacher and student is characterized by an essential asymmetry due to the fact that the teacher holds greater knowledge. The uniqueness of this relationship is expressed

---

17 Talmud, Tractate Sukkah 49b.

18 Talmud, Tractate Avodah Zarah 19a.

19 Ibid.

20 Ibid.

21 Talmud, Tractate Avodah Zarah 35b.

in an analogy between parental and spiritual filiation, which rings true especially when teaching happens in small, intimate settings:[22]

> "And thou shalt teach them diligently unto thy children." (Deuteronomy 6:7) This refers to your disciples, for you find that disciples are always referred to as children, as in the verse: "and the sons of the prophets that were at Bethel came forth to Elisha" (2 Kings 2:3)—were they the children of the prophets? Were they not the disciples? Hence we learn that disciples are called children. Similarly you find that Chezekiah, king of Judah, who taught the entire Torah to Israel, called them his sons, as it is said, "My sons be not now negligent." (2 Chronicles 22:11) Just as sons are called disciples, so the teacher is called father, as it is said, "My father, my father, the chariots of Israel and the horsemen thereof . . ." (2 Kings 2:12)[23]

As in other human relationships, nonverbal dimensions such as body language, intonation, and facial expressions impact communication and, in this case, teaching and learning. Teacher and student do not just happen to be in the same space but are together in a particular way, imbued with implicit expectations, roles, and perceptions, and defined by explicit purposes. It is in the presence of such an adult, and through these various facets of the teaching interaction, that the young person experiences learning, growth, and development. As educational philosopher Max van Manen points out, the teacher-student relationship cannot be reduced to friendship or affection but, rather, should be thought of as a unique type of human relationship.[24]

These different facets show teaching as much more than a practical prelude to a student's learning; it causes a transformation in

---

22 Francoise Waquet insists on this as well. See Francoise Waquet, *Les Enfants de Socrate: Filiation Intellectuelle et Transmission du Savoir, XVIIe-XXIe siècle* (Paris: Albin Michel, 2008). For a discussion of spiritual fatherhood in late antiquity see Peter Brown, *The World of Late Antiquity: from Marcus Aurelius to Muhammad (AD 150–750)* (United Kingdom: Thames and Hudson, 1989).

23 Sifri, 34.

24 Max van Manen, *The Tact of Teaching: Meaning of Pedagogical Thoughtfulness* (London, Ontario: The Althouse Press, 1992), 74.

the learner. Naturally, people who look at teaching focus on the concrete interactions among teacher, students, and subject matter. But the texture of teaching is multidimensional. Teacher and student sense that something takes place in the inner being of each of them and between them. Teaching thus involves a silent awareness of the inter-subjective and the intra-subjective realms.[25] The rabbinic texts discussed in the next three chapters attune teachers and students to a number of these facets within the complexities of teaching and learning.

---

[25] Vygotsky, *Mind in Society*. First comes "inter-subjective" cognitive development, in a social context, and subsequently "intra-subjective" cognitive development, within the individual.

Chapter Five

Learning Transformations

> To educate means to cultivate the soul,
> not only the mind.[1]
>
> —*AJ Heschel*
>
> I am still learning.
>
> —*Michelangelo*

Introduction

Charles L. Brewer was known for his dedication to and for his reflections on the teaching of psychology. In the final sentence of a book chapter about his long and illustrious career, he commented: "I hope the world is a better place because we teachers make a difference to our students; after all, that is what teaching is all about."[2]

Thinking about teaching in terms of making a difference is a little bit like favoring freedom, love, and justice. It meets with general approval from the outset. The use of the idiom "making a difference" links teaching to "making," an action verb that has to do with causation, perhaps even bringing something into being or generating its existence. But it is not at all clear what people mean by this concept, and more clarity about the nature of this

---

[1]   Abraham Joshua Heschel, "The Values of Jewish Education," in *Modern Jewish Educational Thought*, ed. David Wienstein and Michael Yizhar (Chicago: The College of Jewish Studies, 1964), 29.

[2]   Charles L. Brewer, "Reflections on an Academic Career: From Which Side of the Looking Glass?," in *The Teaching of Psychology: Essays in Honor of Wilbert J. McKeachie*, ed. Stephen F. Davis and William Buskist (Mahwah: Erlbaum Brewer, 2002), 507.

"difference" would most probably expose significant variations in the ways people subscribe to the phrase "teaching is about making a difference."

The differences that teachers seek to make often bespeak their philosophical conceptions of teaching. Socrates' midwifery metaphor portrays teaching as assisting in bringing out something that already exists: the understanding of ideas that, according to Socrates' metaphysics, are already latent in the student's soul.[3] Students talk about teachers who have made a difference in their lives. After winning the Nobel Prize for literature in 1957, Albert Camus wrote to Mr. Louis Germain, who had been his elementary school teacher in Algeria:

> I let the commotion around me these days subside a bit before speaking to you from the bottom of my heart. I have just been given far too great an honor, one I neither sought nor solicited. But when I heard the news, my first thought, after my mother, was of you. Without you, without the affectionate hand you extended to the small poor child that I was, without your teaching and example, none of all this would have happened. I don't make too much of this sort of honor. But at least it gives me the opportunity to tell you what you have been and still are for me, and to assure you that your efforts, your work, and the generous heart you put into it still live in one of your little schoolboys who, despite the years, has never stopped being your grateful pupil. I embrace you with all my heart.[4]

In this chapter, three sages discuss quintessential characteristics of teaching Torah through the use of the verb *la'assot* (literally, *to make* or *to do*), in regard to transformations that can, and ideally should, occur in teaching. An analysis of the terms used, the

---

3   Plato, *Theaetetus, The Internet Classics Archive*, trans. Benjamin Jowett, http://classics.mit.edu/Plato/theaetetus.html (148e–151d); and *Menon, The Internet Classics Archive*, trans. Benjamin Jowett, http://classics.mit.edu/Plato/menon.html (lines 80–82).

4   Albert Camus, *The First Man* (New York: Alfred A. Knopf, 1995), 321. Several passages of this book relate Mr. Germain's personal involvement to convince Albert Camus' family that the young Albert should pursue his high school studies rather than join the work market.

selection of proof texts, and the use of literary techniques show that this text is designed to attune the reader and the teacher to a number of experiential aspects which together sketch a few basic lines of a portrait of teaching.

Teaching as Making a Difference
(Talmud, Tractate Sanhedrin 99b)

The Talmud's anonymous editor(s) compiled the views of three different sages, who lived at separate times, to create an instructive text. The three sayings fit one template, as if each of the sages was asked to fill in the blanks. This imagined prompt renders as follow:[5]

(1) _____ (Name) said:

(2) He who teaches Torah to his neighbor's son

(3) is regarded by Scripture as though

(4) he had _____(an essential idea of teaching)

(5) as it is written _____(biblical source that illustrates your statement).

At the outset, the text exposes the characteristic triangle of teaching: the teacher ("He who teaches"), the subject matter ("Torah"), and the student ("his neighbor's son"). The terms are

---

5   This probe can be phrased as a question: "What do you consider the central facet of teaching Torah?" Hans Georg Gadamer's principle of textual interpretation suggests that we understand a text only "when we understand the question to which it is an answer" (Hans-Georg Gadamer, *Truth and Method*, 370). See also Gadamer's "Semantik und Hermeneutik," quoted in Thomas Schwarz Wentzer, "Toward a Phenomenology of Questioning: Gadamer on Questions and Questioning," in *Gadamer's Hermeneutics and the Art of Conversation: International Studies in Hermeneutics and Phenomenology Vol. 2*, ed. Andrzej Wiercinski (Berlin: Lit Verlag, 2011), 246. Also, per Gadamer: "Reconstructing the question, to which the meaning of a text is understood as an answer, merges with our own questioning. For the text must be understood as an answer to a real question" (Gadamer, *Truth and Method*, 374). See also Paul Ricoeur, according to whom reading a text involves looking for "the direction of thought opened up by the text" (Ricoeur, *Interpretation Theory*, 92).

defined: this is a teaching-learning relationship that is not between parent and child. The phrase "is regarded by Scripture as though" is a midrashic idiom that calls attention to something valuable, which he otherwise might miss or underestimate. "Scripture" serves as a normative signpost, inducing the reader to think differently. To that end, the normative reference is personified, providing value judgments and magnifying what ideally should take place in teaching. The comparative expression "as though" reminds us not to take the simile too literally. Finally, the words "as it is written" introduce each sage's scriptural quote, which offers a window into the philosophical underpinnings of his assertion.[6]

Teaching and Student's Transformation

The first teaching is attributed to Resh Lakish,[7] for whom the difference made in teaching Torah resides in the student:

> Resh Lakish said: "He who teaches Torah to his neighbor's son is regarded by Scripture as though he made him."

The Hebrew *assa* literally means "made," though in this context it can be translated as "fashioned." The difference between the active present (He who teaches) and the past-imperfect tenses (he has made him) elicits two emphases in Resh Lakish's saying. The first interpretation underscores the teacher's activity, the process of teaching Torah (He who *teaches* Torah), and the second emphasizes the outcome, following the actual teaching process.[8] The grammatical

---

6   Apparently, the use of present tense (*He who teaches*) reinforces the descriptive meaning of this text, implying that through the very act of teaching Torah, a person is considered "as if he . . ." accomplishes something important, independently of his being cognizant. However, in light of what is described in Chapter Two as reading rabbinical educational texts while being attuned to the texts' potential "awakening" effect on the reader, this text is discussed as reflecting three ideas of what could—and should—ideally characterize the teaching of Torah.

7   See Chapter Four.

8   The text could have used present-imperfect twice: "He who teaches Torah to his neighbor's son is considered by Scripture as though he is making him (*osehu*)."

form blends the two interpretations together and suggests that both the teaching process and what has been learned can lie at the core of the student's transformation. Resh Lakish quotes a biblical passage, "and the souls they made in Charan," based on their common use of the word "made."[9] In its original context, the verse refers to Avraham and Sarah's journey from Charan to Canaan:

> And Avram took Sarai his wife, and Lot his brother's son, and all their possessions that they had gathered, and the souls they *made* in Charan, and they set out to go to the land of Canaan.

The meaning of the phrase "the souls they made in Charan" is not immediately apparent, and its connection to Resh Lakish's teaching is perplexing. The key to this interpretive link resides in a midrashic tradition, as rendered in the following text:

> *And Avram took Sarai his wife, and Lot his brother's son, and all their possessions that they had gathered, and the souls they made in Charan.* (Genesis 12:5) Rabbi Elazar observed in the name of Rabbi Yossi the son of Zimra: "If all the nations assembled to create one insect they could not endow it with life, yet you say *and the souls they made in Charan*! It refers, however, to the proselytes. Then let it say 'that they converted.' Why *they made*? That is to teach you that he who brings a gentile near [to God] and converts him is as though he created him."[10]

The midrash describes Avraham and Sarah as converting people to monotheism prior to their leaving Charan to go to the Promised Land, and this is the reference to "the souls they made in Charan." Particularly relevant to Resh Lakish's teaching is the association of the words "making," "creation," and "conversion." According to the midrash, the Bible chooses the verb "made," instead of the verb "converted," to underscore people's experience of a renewed creation of themselves, since the word "made" refers to the creation of the world in Genesis. The midrash seems to intentionally blur

---

9   Genesis, 12:5.

10   Bereishit Rabba, Lech Lecha, 39: 14.

the distinction between the biological creation of beings and the metaphorical use of creation as a personal and subjective experience to emphasize a sense of new being. In the literary context of this midrash, "conversion" is a figure of speech, not a formal change of religion. It connotes a deep shift in a person's experience of self and a reorientation of meaning in regard to things that deeply matter, as widely discussed in modern psychology.[11] Resh Lakish wants such transformation to be on the teacher's mind as he sets out to teach Torah.[12] He expresses his view from within a sort of twilight zone between his experience as a teacher and his experience as a student. While the text seems to emphasize the teacher's perspective (*He who teaches*), the name of the speaker and the proof text emphasizing existential transformation send the reader back to Resh Lakish's

---

[11]   Raymond F. Paloutzian, "Psychology of Religious Conversion and Spiritual Transformation," in *The Oxford Handbook of Religious Conversion*, ed. Lewis R. Rambo and Charles E. Farhadian, New York: Oxford Handbooks Online, 2014), http://www.oxfordhandbooks.com.

[12]   Pierre Hadot, a historian of antique and Greek philosophy, discusses the concept of conversion by retracing its etymology. The Latin word *conversio* corresponds to two different words in Ancient Greek: *epistrophè*, implying the idea of a return (return to an origin; a turn to one's inner soul), and *metanoia*, which means "change of thought" or "repentance," implying the idea of a mutation and rebirth; see Pierre Hadot, *Exercices Spirituels et Philosophie Antique* (Paris: Albin Michel 2002), 223. Relevant to Resh Lakish's own experience (further discussed in Chapter Four of this book), is Hadot's discussion of conversion caused by philosophy. It is experienced as a tearing off and a rupture from the day-to-day, from the familiar; a return to the authentic and to the essential, a radical new beginning that changes the person's perception of the past as well as of the future. Conversion causes a sense of internal liberty, a new conception of the world and an access to authentic existence; see ibid., 233–234. In modern literature, we are reminded of William James' description of conversion: "To be converted, to be regenerated, to receive grace, to experience religion, to gain an assurance, are so many phrases which denote the process, gradual or sudden, by which a self hitherto divided, and consciously wrong inferior and unhappy, becomes unified and consciously right superior and happy, in consequence of its firmer hold upon religious realities. This at least is what conversion signifies in general terms, whether or not we believe that a direct divine operation is needed to bring such a moral change about" (William James, *The Varieties of Religious Experience: A Study in Human Nature, Being the Gifford Lectures on Natural Religion Delivered at Edinburgh in 1901–1902* [London: Longman, Greens and Co., 1902], 89).

own experience as described in the Talmud (see Chapter Four).[13] Only someone who has experienced firsthand this kind of transformative effect of learning Torah is capable of pointing to it as an essential element of teaching. This view of teaching as a "making" of the student manifests something of the teacher's sense of her vocation in a broader view of cultural transmission. The nature of the change encompasses the student's personality, expanding true learning beyond a simple acquisition of knowledge. But the text does not provide a more refined understanding of the nature of this transformation nor concrete examples. The lack of further specificity characterizes all three sayings of this Talmudic text and has further implications.

Teaching and the Innovation of Torah

The second utterance of this Talmudic text is by Rabbi Elazar the son of Arach, a late first-century CE sage and one of the leading figures of rabbinic Judaism following the destruction of the Temple. Rabbi Elazar is described by his teacher, Rabbi Yochanan the son of Zakkai, as an ever-increasing wellspring (k'maayan hamitgaber) — a metaphor for a bottomless font of creative teachings.[14] Rabbi Elazar's creative abilities are echoed in what he values at the very heart of teaching:

> Rabbi Elazar said: "He who teaches Torah to his neighbor's son is regarded by Scripture as though he himself made the words of the Torah."

The words of the Torah already exist, but Rabbi Elazar's metaphor conveys the idea of new meaning being generated from the words of the Torah themselves. In his commentary, Rabbi Adin Steinsaltz writes "as though he himself is the generator of Torah," referring to the explicit expression of new ideas that hadn't been articulated until then. Rabbi Elazar does not refer to a pre-existing

---

13   Talmud, Tractate Baba Metzia 84a–84b, as discussed at length in Chapter Four.

14   *Ethics of the Fathers*, Chapter 2: 8.

meaning, already known by people, which the teacher happens to discover for the first time during his teaching. Rabbi Elazar implies that the new meaning is objectively new, not only to the teacher but in the universe of Torah learning. New understandings would seem more likely among advanced Talmud students.[15] Unexpectedly, however, Rabbi Elazar places this creative facet in the context of a teacher with a young student, thereby emphasizing the potential creative dimension that resides in the very act of teaching.

This view conveys three ideas: The teacher remains open to the unexpected and to new insights; teaching is a dynamic and interactive process, wherein both teacher and student are prepared, engaged, and receptive; and, finally, that there is something about the nature of teaching, the act of putting ideas in words for another person, the effort to "translate" the ideas in a way that might be conducive for student's learning, that provides the conditions necessary for the emergence of new insights. Rabbi Elazar's idea reflects an intuition about teaching as a peculiar way of gaining knowledge or insight, wherein understanding comes only through the action itself. It is reminiscent of early twentieth-century philosopher Robin George Collingwood's description of painting:

> You see something in your subject, of course, before you begin to paint it . . . but only a person with experience of painting, and of painting well, can realize how little that is, compared with what you come to see in it as your painting progresses.[16]

For Collingwood there are two aspects to painting: cognition (knowing or seeing) and activity (painting), and each is conditional upon the other. "Only a person who paints can see well; and conversely."[17] Like Resh Lakish, Rabbi Elazar is not specific; he does not explain how to achieve such innovations. A close examination of his choice of a scriptural passage, taken from Moses' late sermon

15   See discussion in Introduction to Part Two.

16   Robin G. Collingwood, *The Principles of Art* (Oxford: Oxford University Press, 1958), 303.

17   Ibid., 304.

to the Israelites, provides additional insight: "Keep therefore the words of this covenant, and do [literally, *accomplish*] them, that you may prosper in all that you do."[18]

In its original scriptural context, "do them" (*va'assitem otam*) refer to the words of the covenant, i.e., "accomplish the commandments." Rabbi Elazar, however, takes advantage of a second meaning of the verb "doing" to interpret this phrase in an unconventional sense as "making them" (in the sense of "fashioning them"), and "the words of this covenant" as referring not to the commandments but to all the words of the Torah. *Prima facie*, any connection between the meaning of this biblical verse and the activity of teaching is invisible. The key to Rabbi Elazar's teaching resides in the exegetical shift he performs in his unconventional reading—by which he actually demonstrates a radical example of what it means to "fashion new words of Torah." What he says outwardly—on the surface of his assertion—is what he is doing internally within his reinterpretation. Fashioning the words of Torah while teaching requires genuine openness to the polysemous nature of the written word, and in turn to new semantic meanings of Scripture.[19] Such openness, Rabbi Elazar believes, should characterize a person's attitude toward Scripture, and thus also a teacher's stance when the fresh eye of youth is engaged in the study of Torah.[20]

---

[18]   Deuteronomy, 29:8.

[19]   Closer to our time, we find in Hasidic literature similar thoughts about the learner's semantic openness, and the language's flexibility, as a key idea for creative learning. Consider the following example: "And they set forward from the mount of God three days' journey" (Numbers 10:33). A midrashic tradition interprets these three days as one long flight, "as a child who leaves school and runs" (Yalkut Shimoni, Numbers, paragraph 729). In a slightly different version: "They were fleeing away from Mount Sinai for three days because they had studied a lot of Torah at Mount Sinai" (Tosafot in Talmud, Tractate Shabbat 116a). Rabbi Yosef Ruzin (1858–1936), known as *the Rogatchover*, attributes the Israelites' flight to the fact that they only wanted to learn the words of the Torah but were not ready to learn its letters (Rabbi Yosef Ruzin, *Tsafnat Pa-aneach Vol. 4* [Jerusalem: Tsafnat Pa-anech Institute, 1962], 110).

[20]   Kathy Shultz, *Listening: A Framework for Teaching Across Differences* (New York and London: Teacher College Press, 2003); Michael Welton, "Listening,

Teaching and Teachers' Transformation

Rabbi Abba the son of Yoseph bar Chama, known as Rava, headed one of the great Babylonian Talmudic academies in Mechoza (circa 280–352 CE). He is an oft-cited sage and is described as someone who attracted many students, which probably attests to personal charisma.[21] For Rava, the author of the third quote in our Talmudic passage, the difference made through the teaching of Torah occurs within the teacher:

> Rava said: "He who teaches Torah to his neighbor's son is regarded by Scripture as though he made himself."

This emphasis is rather unusual, as discussions of teaching are usually geared toward the experience of the student and/or the curricular subject matter. Rava is attempting to attune the teacher to a subtle dimension of his vocation. The formulation "as though he made himself" implies growth, a process of coming into being, and identity development. Teaching encompasses intentional and practical acts that seek to assist someone else in his learning, but Rava is pointing to a relationship in which the teacher's personality can be altered. Again, there is no further clarification, so the nature of this transformation and the conditions conducive to such an experience remain elusive.

Rava draws on the same verse in Deuteronomy as Rabbi Elazar. He adopts an exegetical principle that is common in rabbinic literature, building on the fact that Scripture does not

---

Conflict and Citizenship: Towards a Pedagogy of Civil Society," *International Journal of Lifelong Education* 21 (2002): 197–208; Clark Thomas, "Sharing the Importance of Attentive Listening Skills," *Journal of Management Education* 23 (1999): 216–223; Vivian G. Palley, "On Listening to What Children Say," *Harvard Educational Review* 56 (1986): 122–131. More recently, *Teacher College Record* has dedicated a special issue to listening in the context of teaching and learning: *Teachers College Record* 112, no. 11 (2010). Listening is central to learning, yet only recently have education researchers recognized its more complex and challenging aspects. Also see Holzer with Kent, *A Philosophy of Havruta*, 106–122.

[21]   Talmud, Tractate Ta'anit 9a.

show the dots and lines that dictate which vowels are pronounced among the written, visible consonants. Vowels have the power to change the meaning of the words significantly. Rava changes two vowels, transforming "and do them" (*va'assitem* **ot**a*m*) into "and do you[rselves]" (*va'assitem* **at**e*m*). Outwardly, in their black-on-white appearance, the words that Rava brings to bolster his point are exactly the same as those brought by Rabbi Elazar. However, his exegetical strategy may hold the key: Rava is attuned to the non-graphical, invisible aspect of the written Torah—the vowels—to make the teacher aware of an aspect of teaching that remains by and large invisible and is the least talked about: the teacher's inner change through and in the experience of teaching.[22] Rava's biblical reference suggests that his flexibility in swapping the vowels— the non-graphical, inner dimension of the biblical words—echoes the inner flexibility needed for the teacher to be transformed in and through the dynamic implied in teaching Torah to a young student. This idea may have a special valence if an experienced teacher sees himself as the all-knowing adult who is transmitting his knowledge to the younger student, thus *a priori* not expecting anything significant to happen to him.

Is this experiential transformation caused by the Torah concepts that are being taught? Or inspired by the relational experience of teaching a young student? Rava's saying does not provide enough information to address those questions. A more comprehensive reading of the entire text may elucidate its deeper meaning.

A Threefold Transformation

Each of the three sages provides only scant explanation of his respective view of teaching-related transformation. At the same time, the lack of specificity evokes the transformative potential of teaching as an overarching dimension. By their very nature, transformations take very different, and at times subtle, forms. The verb "make"

---

22   The teachings of both Rabbi Elazar and Rava are echoed in another rabbinic text that discusses the performance of mitzvot. See Midrash Tanchuma, Deuteronomy 1.

(*assa*) affirms a cluster of ideas. In addition, dynamic changes are not necessarily palpable in concrete instances of teaching, and they may be among the human experiences that cannot be articulated. The three sayings awaken the reader/teacher's awareness of what David Hawkins calls the teacher's "diagnostic role" in regard to the three elements of the learning interaction: the subject matter, the student's, and the teacher's actions.

A similar idea is conveyed through the literary structure of this text, created through the merging of the three separate sayings into a matched, parallel set. The redactor did not quote the three sages in chronological order, choosing instead to cite third-century scholar Resh Lakish first, followed by first-century scholar Rabbi Elazar, and concluding with fourth-century scholar Rava. This suggests purposeful editorial crafting.

The text's echoes of David Hawkins' instructional triangle go beyond the triangular paradigm of *who* teaches *what* to *whom*. While focusing on the student's learning, the Talmudic text expands the transformation to include the subject matter and the teacher. The recurring template has a double effect: it sets out each saying separately, yet also integrates them. This literary form may be intended to lead to the conclusion that, ideally, teaching transforms all three: student, subject matter, and teacher. Similarly, folding the three sayings into one template increases their potential interconnectedness and suggests their reciprocal impact: each of them is essential to the instance of teaching ("He who teaches Torah to his neighbor's son"), and each may cause a transformation in either or both of the others. Finally, by preserving all three of these opinions and by not judging any one of them as more essential than the others, the edited text may acknowledge that it is not necessary or perhaps not desirable to embrace one type of transformation more than the others.

Learning Transformations: Contemporary Resonances

Since the 1970s and under the influence of the work of sociologist Jack Mezirow, transformative learning has become a rich and complex concept in the literature of educational research, with increasingly refined understandings of what it entails and its implications for instruction.[23] It is a theory-based educational method grounded in cognitive and developmental psychology.[24] It underscores transformation in three dimensions: psychological (understanding of the self), convictional (belief systems), and behavioral (lifestyle).[25]

In contrast, the Talmudic text discussed in this chapter provides only a primary awareness of transformations that may occur during or following teaching. But it also projects an elementary consciousness, a type of appeal reminiscent of Ludwig Wittgenstein's call in the realm of epistemology: "Back to the rough ground!" No doubt, the fruits of scholarly investigations on transformative learning and its practical implementations on instruction continue to make an important contribution to educational theory and instructional practice. Yet, at times, there is a need to be called

---

[23] Jack Mezirow, "Perspective Transformation," *Adult Education Quarterly* 28, no. 2 (1978): 100–110; Jack Mezirow, "Transformative Learning: Theory to Practice," *New Directions for Adult and Continuing Education* 74 (1997): 5–12; Jack Mezirow and Associates, *Learning as Transformation* (San Francisco: Jossey-Bass, 2000). Other psychological schools of thoughts have come to bear on transformative learning as well: John M. Dirkx, "Nurturing Soul Work: A Jungian Approach to Transformative Learning," in *The Handbook of Transformative Learning: Theory, Research, and Practice*, ed. Patricia C. Cranton and Edward W. Taylor (Hoboken: John Wiley & Sons, 2012), 116–129. For elaborated theoretical views on transformation in regard to teaching and learning, see for example, John M. Dirkx, "Transformative Learning Theory in the Practice of Adult Education: An Overview," *PAACE Journal of Lifelong Learning* 7 (1998): 1–14. Robert Kegan defines information as new skills or knowledge that a person acquires to keep up with new needs and demands, which therefore is helpful but does not contribute to growth. In contrast, transformation changes the very "form" of the person who knows, making him more able to deal with uncertainty and more complex realities. According to Kegan, transformative learning happens when a person changes, "not just the way he behaves, not just the way he feels, but the way he knows—not just what he knows but the *way* he knows" (Kegan, *In Over Our Heads*, 17).

[24] John M. Dirkx, "Transformative Learning Theory in the Practice of Adult Education: An Overview," 1–14.

[25] David Elias, "It's Time to Change Our Minds: An Introduction to Transformative Learning," *ReVision* 20, no. 1 (1997): 2–6.

back to the basics of teaching, especially in the wake of educational orientations that conceptualize teaching as being concerned only with the transmission of information, and which embrace technical views of teaching on the basis of what they perceive as its practical effectivity.[26] In contrast, this text calls for a type of elementary attentiveness and a genuine openness to the possibility that teaching affects the student, the subject matter, and the teacher herself. It implies the need for a critical examination of uncritical reliance on methodology and of all-encompassing theoretical frameworks that conceptualize teaching as technical knowledge.[27]

Scientism may become a sweeping ideology of adopting an empirical approach that sees all phenomena through the lens of a problem waiting to be solved. "A genuine problem is subject to an appropriate technique," writes existentialist philosopher Gabriel Marcel (1889–1973).[28] To attend to a student's learning solely through the lens of *problem* places her learning as an object that lies before the teacher as a problem to which she must lay siege, solve, and master. *Mystery* refers to the palpable aspects of human experience that transcend every conceivable technique. The mysterious should not be confused with the unknowable but is "a sphere where the distinction between what is in me and what is before me loses its meaning and its initial validity."[29] The recognition of mystery entails a positive act of the mind, especially in the context of teaching. By linking teaching to the verb "to make," and pointing to the student, the subject matter, and the teacher herself as locus of transformation, the Talmudic text invites a renewed awareness that

---

[26] Dunne, *Back to the Rough Ground.*

[27] Hans-Georg Gadamer, *Truth and Method*, 325: "The hermeneutical consciousness has its fulfillment, not in the methodological awareness of itself, but in the same readiness for experience that distinguishes the experienced man by comparison with the man captivated by dogma."

[28] Gabriel Marcel, *Being and Having* (Westminster: Dacre Press, 1949), 117.

[29] Ibid. The distinction between problem and mystery as two fundamental attitudes and as a key for a critique of the technical cultural orientations of Western culture is echoed in Martin Heidegger's distinction between "calculative" and "meditative" thinking (Martin Heidegger, *Discourse on Thinking* [New York: Harper Torchbooks, 1969]).

can rejuvenate the teacher's open and curious attitude toward the intra- and intersubjective aspects of teaching and learning, and lead to new or old perspectives on the moral grounds of teaching.[30]

---

[30]   See Chapter Eight, the section *Teachers' Attuned Teaching*.

Chapter Six

DISRUPTIONS AND REPAIRS

Through the Thou a person becomes I
—*Martin Buber*

Introduction

Think of yourself as a learner: What do you do when, during class, circumstances cause you to "shut down"? When something in a text or with a learning partner either offends you or distances you, how do you usually react? How do you reconnect after such moments?

This question appears in a pre-course assignment, which asks participants to describe their dispositions as learners before a five-day education seminar. There may be disruptions in essential learning relationships among the teacher, the student, and the content.[1] One participant, "Sally," reported that she disconnected following an unconscious, offhand comment by an instructor. Sally shut down but concealed her experience. If not for the alertness of another instructor who, later that day, sensed Sally's unrest and reached out to her, she probably would not have returned to the seminar the following day. In retrospect, Sally recounted, "I was no longer positioned to learn from him," and that she "could not listen."[2] Since then, participants are asked to write about disconnection and

---

1   Miriam Raider-Roth, Vicki Stieha, and Billy Hensley, "Rupture and Repair: Episodes of Resistance and Resilience in Teachers' Learning," *Teaching and Teacher Education* 28 (2012): 493–502; Holzer with Kent, *A Philosophy of Havruta*, 67–71.

2   Raider-Roth, Stieha, and Hensley, "Rupture and Repair," 498.

reconnection before their seminars. According to the faculty, this pedagogical device prepares them "for the idea that disconnections can happen and are part of the learning process."[3]

Relational disconnections are inevitable. In the dynamic classroom, teachers' and learners' interactions are in constant flux, nurtured by conscious or less conscious perceptions and misperceptions, assumptions, expectations, and strong feelings. Sally is a veteran English teacher and administrator, and a collaborative and collegial leader. She experienced a deep disconnect despite the fact that the comment was not addressed to her or to anyone specific. Neither in her perception of the learning environment, nor in herself, could Sally find an anchor, that might have helped her engage in repairing the broken relationship. Without such essential repair, no learning is likely to occur. Inspired by relational psychology theories, recent educational research seeks to raise teachers' awareness of students' disruptions and offer both conceptual and practical tools designed to help teachers re-engage students in learning.[4] But what about students' self-awareness and their ability to relate to disruptions in learning relationships with teachers and/or subject matter? What practical support could be offered to initiate repair of relationships in the educational context? This chapter fuels thinking about these questions, utilizing an ancient rabbinic text.

Dull Iron and Fractured Relationships
(Midrash Rabba on Ecclesiastes 10:10)[5]

According to the book of Ecclesiastes, even a small amount of foolishness can cause a fair amount of damage. One of its examples serves as springboard for our text:

---

3   Ibid., 501.

4   Dawn Skorczewski, *Teaching One Moment at a Time: Disruption and Repair in the Classroom* (Amherst: University of Massachusetts Press, 2005).

5   Ecclesiastes Rabba is an aggadic commentary on Ecclesiastes. It includes a compilation of earlier Talmudic and midrashic sources and is estimated to have been edited between the sixth and the eighth century. .

> If the iron (axe) be dull, and one does not whet the edge,
> then he must apply more strength; but wisdom is profitable
> to direct.[6]

Cutting with a blunt tool would require much more force. A common workman must be wise enough to stop and sharpen his axe, lest he waste energy and possibly put himself in danger. Thus the wisdom resides in whetting the edge as needed. However, the surrounding verses in the tenth chapter of Ecclesiastes talk about the ignoramus, which leads to an interpretation that only greater wisdom can improve an ignoramus' situation.[7] The midrash extends the meaning metaphorically to breakdowns of student-teacher relationships, as experienced by students. Wisdom, then, consists of taking responsibility for the repair of the relationship. The midrash offers three interpretations of this verse, to discuss three instances of disruption and repair. In each interpretation, it divides the verse into segments and changes some words' literal meaning significantly. Also, the midrash's interpretive work delves into the nuances of the Hebrew words *vehu lo panim*, which is rendered as "one does not whet the edge" but which more literally means "and he does not have a face." The word *panim* alludes to the human face, and particularly according to this midrash, to the teacher's face.[8]

---

6   אם קהה הברזל והוא לא פנים קלקל וחילים יגבר ויתרון הכשיר חכמה 10:10 Ecclesiastes
The New Jewish Public Society's translation renders: "If the axe has become dull and he has not whetted the edge, he must exert more strength. Thus the advantage of a skill [depends on the exercise of] prudence."

7   Ecclesiastes, 10:10; *Daat Mikra* (Jerusalem: Mossad Harav Kook, 1973).

8   Talmud, Tractate Ta'anit 7b–8a provides a number of different midrashic interpretations on Ecclesiastes 10:10. Resh Lakish uses it to address the need to invest effort in the systematic organization of one's knowledge, without which (as Rashi explains) topics gets confused and legal deduction is affected: Resh Lakish said: If you see a student for whom his studies are as hard as iron, it is because he has failed to systematize his studies, as it is said, "And one does not whet the edge." What is his remedy? Let him attend the school even more regularly, as it is said, "Then must he put to more strength; but wisdom is profitable to direct." [The latter words indicate] how much more profitable his efforts would be if he had originally systematized his studies (Talmud, Tractate Ta'anit 7b-8a).

First Interpretation: An Uncaring Teacher

The midrash reads the verse by interpreting its different fragments:

> "If the iron (axe) be blunt," if the teacher becomes dull toward his student, like iron
> "and one does not whet the edge (and he does not show face)," and the teacher does not show a bright countenance to him,
> "spoilt," deterioration of conduct will result in the student
> "then he must apply more strength," let the student bring ten people who should appease the teacher,
> "but wisdom is profitable to direct," so that finally he will cause the rightness of wisdom to prevail.[9]

In this midrash's first teaching, the student experiences his teacher as having become insensitive toward him. Consequently, the student's behavior will deteriorate. What should the student do? He should bring ten people who will appease the teacher and so he will cause the rightness of wisdom to prevail.

The text invites the reader into the student's subjective experience. In rabbinic literature, the Hebrew expression *lehasbir panim* conveys two different meanings. On one hand, it evokes a strong affective connotation, as it refers to a person's welcoming face.[10] *Panim* can also refer to the figurative "face" of the subject matter, giving rise to a cognitive-didactic meaning: the explanation of the subject matter.[11] Here, in this midrash, it is the former: the student experiences a breakdown in the "I-Thou" interpersonal interaction.[12] It is not that the teacher fails to explain the material

---

9   Midrash Rabba, Ecclesiastes 10:10. The Hebrew version renders as follows:
אם קהה הברזל, אם נתקהה הרב על התלמיד כברזל, והוא לא פנים, ואין הרב מסביר פנים לתלמיד, קלקל,
קלקול מעשים יש בתלמיד, וחילים יגבר, מה יעשה יביא עשרה בני אדם והם מפייסין את הרב, סוף שהוא מותיר
הכשר חכמה.

10   *Ethics of the Fathers,* 1: 15

11   Ibid., 3: 11; Talmud, Tractate Sanhedrin 93b.

12   In the second midrash's teaching, the text says *ve-ein harav masbir,* "and the teacher does not explain." The omission of the word "face" clearly indicates that in this case the teacher does not shed light on the subject matter, and it therefore makes more sense to interpret the first saying the way I suggest. This interpretation echoes Talmud, Tractate Ta'anit 8a: Rava said: If you see

well. Nor is the teacher expressing personal animosity toward a particular student. The midrash alludes to the absence of what David Hawkins describes as the teacher's "diagnostic" disposition toward a student's learning, a presence that takes the form of an intentional and proactive caring.[13] The teacher may objectively be doing his job, but the student experiences him as lethargic, lacking, and cold, like blunt iron—an animosity that is captured by the midrash in the non-radiant face. No timeframe of the student's experience is provided by the midrash. Most likely, the rupture has built up over time, excluding the case of a student's caprice, or an isolated bad experience. Also noticeable is the absence of reason for the teacher's insufficiency. As a literary effect, this suggests not only that different causes are possible, but that the causes are secondary to the main idea of this text. Nor does it matter if the student's experience reflects the reality of the teacher's behavior or only his own feelings. What the midrash highlights is the student's subjective experience. Moreover, the concern does not seem to be the impact on the student's academic achievements, but his conduct vis-à-vis the teacher and perhaps even more, outside the classroom and in the future.[14] Torah study possesses a vocational aspect, designed to be formative for a student's life.[15] The connection established between the lack of the teacher's bright countenance and the student's behavior reflects a vision about the

---

a student who finds his studies as hard as iron, it is because his teacher does not show him bright countenance [*eino masbir lo panim*], as it is said, "and one does not whet the edge."

[13] Hawkins, "I, Thou, It," 55.

[14] The midrash renders: *Kilkul ma'asim yesh batalmid* literally: "deterioration of actions is in the student," (Midrash Rabba, Ecclesiastes 10:10.) This may be "bad classroom behavior." The use of the present tense *yesh* ("is") does not preclude a concern for the future, especially because the midrash uses the word *ma'asim*, actions or deeds, including moral behavior as well as ritual-oriented religious conduct. In rabbinic literature, the term "conduct" does not distinguish between the moral and the religious, and thus in the lack of further textual indication, I understand the midrash as concerned with both.

[15] See Introduction to Part Three and Chapter Five.

educational scope of teaching to include nonverbal dimensions as well.[16]

The midrash suggests that the repair process should begin with the student reaching out to "ten people who appease the teacher, so that he will cause the rightness of wisdom to prevail."[17] In rabbinic tradition, the minimum of ten (male) adults is the required quorum for an official assembly. The midrash's exhortation implies two important statements. First, it instructs the student to initiate a process of repair, thereby highlighting the student's responsibility toward his own learning but also toward the repair process. Second, by calling upon the broader community's intervention, the midrash conveys the moral obligation of the community regarding education, and the teacher's broader accountability toward the community. Teaching Torah is not conceptualized as the teacher's private business. Rabbinic tradition rules that it is mandatory for communities to provide their children with an opportunity for Torah study, and the community as a whole is responsible for the installation of teachers.[18] The task of the assembled committee is not to blame, let alone to fire, but to "appease the teacher" so that he will recover his full commitment to the student's learning. According to the midrash, when this repair is achieved, it is "the rightness of wisdom" that prevails.

Second Interpretation: A Disgruntled Teacher

The second midrashic teaching changes the facts of the case:

---

[16] This idea is discussed in Chapter Five.

[17] In the situation discussed by Rava (Talmud, Tractate Ta'anit 8a, see Footnote 12), the student is called to mobilize companions who will appease the teacher: "What is his remedy? Let him seek many companions [to intercede for him with his teacher], as it is said. Then must he put to more strength; but wisdom is profitable to direct. [The latter words indicate] how much more successful he would have been had his efforts originally found favor with his teacher."

[18] Talmud, Baba Batra 21a; Maimonides, Laws of Torah Study, 2: 2; Joseph Karo, *Shulchan Aruch, Yoreh Deah*, 245: 7–8.

If the iron (axe) be blunt, if the student has been blunt [i.e., annoying] to his teacher [by his obtuseness], as it is said "Iron sharpens iron" (Proverbs 27:17), and [as a result] *and one does not whet the edge,* the teacher does not explain [the subject matter] to the student, *spoilt,* deterioration of conduct will result in the student. *Then must he put to more strength,* let [the student] bring ten men and they will appease his teacher. *But wisdom is profitable to direct,* so that the teacher will abandon his anger and direct the student's learning.[19]

In this instance, the student has been annoying, and as a result experiences a rupture in the attitude of the teacher, who fails or refuses to explain the material to him. Unlike in the first teaching, the student feels responsible for the teacher's disconnect, and the teacher's animosity is therefore also perceived as intentional and personal. The erosion in the relationship is expressed metaphorically by the verse from Proverbs, "Iron sharpens iron,"[20] which alludes to the reciprocal engagement of learners and teachers with the subject matter, a mutual sharpening that is central to learning.[21] Again, the immediate and long-term concern of the midrash relates to the student's conduct, implying that lack of Torah study might jeopardize the student's growth. Therefore, the teacher's anger cannot prevail, and an initiative toward healing the rupture must be introduced. As in the previous case, it is the student's obligation to alert the broader community. Contemporary readers may wonder why the student is not encouraged to apologize and thus appease the teacher. Beyond historical cultural values, this may reflect the emphasis on the community's responsibility for the teaching of Torah.[22]

---

[19] The original Hebrew version renders as follows:

אם קהה הברזל: אם נתקהה התלמיד על הרב שנאמר (משלי כז) ברזל בברזל יחד ואין הרב מסביר לתלמיד, קלקל, קלקול מעשים יש בתלמיד, וחילים יגבר, ילך ויביא עשרה בני אדם ויפייסין את רבו, ויתרון הכשר חכמה, סוף הוא מותיר לו כעסו ויכשיר לו את תלמודו.

[20] Proverbs 27:17

[21] See Introduction to Part Two.

[22] While there also are potential downsides in the repair process recommended by the midrash, from a modern psychological perspective, there also could be

Third Interpretation: An Incompetent Teacher

If the iron (axe) be blunt: If the study has been hard to you like iron *and one does not whet the edge*, and he [your teacher] does not come to you to make it clear for you, then denounce him with all your might.[23]

Now it is the subject matter that has become dull. The midrash does not address the particular topic the student is having trouble understanding. It is studying as a whole that has become hard like iron as the student experiences a disconnection from the subject matter. An extra investment of effort would not help; the problem is not that the material is too challenging. Like a blunt axe, the student is not finding the resources and the means to "cut through" the density of the subject matter. The drama, however, is that the teacher is not helpful: "and he [your teacher] does not come to you to make it clear for you."[24] This expression refers to a lack of personal effort and concern, as well as a lack of ability to make the material understandable to this particular student. The student is experiencing a triple disconnect: his own rupture vis-à-vis the subject matter, the teacher's lack of effort, and the teacher's ineptitude. In such cases, the midrash enjoins the student to "denounce him with all your might." Again, the student is expected to react to the teacher's failure. The midrash does not specify the audience for such denunciation. Perhaps the student should alert the community, or maybe he is to break the ban of silence with anyone who should know. Also, the midrash does not mention appeasement and repair, yet it also does not say that the teacher would be dismissed. This lack of detail allows the reader to infer

---

benefits in having a third player involved as the community's representative. It may, for example, be helpful for inhibited students who would rather stay in a state of disconnect than enter a confrontation. It may also avoid unhealthy power relationships that are more likely to occur between teacher and student when nobody else is involved.

[23] The original Hebrew renders as follows:
אם קהה הברזל - אם נקהה תלמודך עליך כברזל, והוא לא פנים קלקל אינו בא לידך להסבירו בפניך, קלקל עליו בחילך.

[24] אינו בא לידיך להסבירו לפניך

that in extreme cases of incompetency, the teacher should be kept from teaching, as he fails to keep his most essential commitment, which is to mediate the subject matter for the student's learning.

Assisting Students in Repair

What happens when a student feels his learning is obstructed, and he cannot proceed without the teacher's assistance? Ideally, we expect the teacher to recognize the issue and to act accordingly. Alternately, we expect the student to reach out to his teacher and ask for help. But what if instead of the pathway to a solution, the student perceives the teacher to be the origin of the problem and thus unapproachable? The midrash uses four ways to assist this student.

First, the midrash provides words and images describing similar circumstances, which may help the student become self-aware regarding his experience of a disruption. This effect is reinforced by the fact that the midrash refrains from casting any doubt on the student's perception. Instead, it relates to his experience as valid *prima facie*. David Hawkins' model of the instructional triangle (renamed as the *relational triangle*[25]) can be adapted to provide a conceptual representation of the three situations discussed by the midrash. As discussed in Chapter One, Hawkins seeks to raise the teacher's awareness of her role in the triangular interaction of teacher, learner, and subject matter in which learning happens. While the teacher participates in the reciprocal interaction among the three players, she is labeled by Hawkins as the self-aware "I," because she is the one who simultaneously is cognizant of her interaction with student and subject matter while also stimulating it by her actions. In contrast, in the midrash, it is the student who is self-aware regarding his experience and who is summoned to take action. Consequently, I label the student here as the *I* who interacts with the teacher (*Thou*) and with the subject matter (*It*).

---

[25]   Raider-Roth and Holzer, "Learning to be Present."

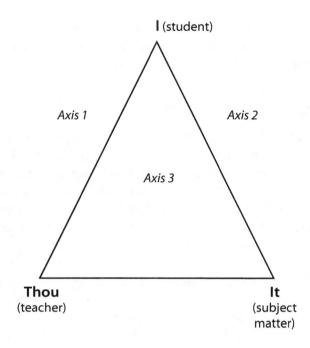

Figure 1: **The relational triangle implied in the midrash.**

Hawkins insists that a genuine student-teacher relationship greatly depends on reciprocal confidence and trust.[26] The midrash facilitates the student's becoming aware of instances in which he experiences a rupture in his basic confidence toward the teacher. In the first instance, the rupture is located on Axis 1: the student experiences a perceived absence of his teacher's interest in him as a learner. In the second instance, the disruption is again experienced on Axis 1, but also as forestalling the teacher's leading of the student to the subject matter's comprehension (Axis 2). Finally, in the midrash's third instance, the student perceives a rupture between the teacher and the subject matter (Axis 3), which then precludes its mediation for the student (Axis 2), and, consequently, also the rupture between teacher and student, given the teacher's lack of care.

---

26   Hawkins, "I, Thou and It," 56.

The student is made aware of his responsibility through the depiction of the first case, in which he has no sense of what may have caused the teacher's animosity, and the second case, in which he has reasons to blame himself. In both cases, the midrash insists the student should not simply endure the deficiency in his learning. Furthermore, the midrash offers the student practical injunctions: to mobilize the community and, in the third case, to denounce the teacher. Finally, the entire midrash empowers the student to act in the face of such disrupted relationships and by the same token insists on making him the primary party responsible for his own learning when the teacher is perceived as the problem and not the solution.

These insights are reinforced by two literary features: the three instances are presented anonymously and are introduced with the expression "another interpretation."[27] From a phenomenological point of view, this reinforces a sense that the midrash is expressing the view of a single voice, which, through the cumulative effect of the three sayings, highlights what each conveys individually as well as the text's message as an integrated unit.

The midrash adds an additional scenario of student disconnect by way of a story:

> One of the students of Rabbi Shimon bar Yochai forgot his learning; so he went weeping to the cemetery. After he had wept much, [his teacher] appeared to him in his dream and said to him: "When you throw three pebbles at me I will come." The student went to an interpreter of dreams and related to him what had occurred. He told him, "Repeat your lesson three times and it will come to you [so that you will not forget it]." He did this, and so it happened to him.[28]

From the solution offered, we understand that the student still remembers segments of what he learned from his teacher,

---

[27] דבר אחר

[28] חד מתלמידיו דרבי שמעון בר יוחאי אינשי אולפניה. אזל ליה בכי לבי עולמין, מדכי הוה בכי סגי אתחמי ליה בחלמיה, ואמר ליה כד תהא רמי בי תלתא קלי אנא אתי, אזיל ההוא תלמידא לגבי פתר חילמייא ותני ליה עובדא, אמר ליה אמור פירקך תלת זימנין והוא אתי לך, ועבד כן וכן הות ליה.

and the midrash suggests that going over what is already known might generate an associative process that helps retrieve additional information. This section evokes ideas implied in the previous sections regarding ruptures and repair. Here, the student's forgotten Torah is connected to the longing for his teacher, whose death caused their disconnection. The student weeps in the cemetery. Is he yearning for the Torah he forgot, or for his teacher? The midrash subtly blurs the distinction between these two absences in the parallel between the teacher's allegorical advice ("When you throw three pebbles at me I will come") and its practical interpretation ("Repeat your lesson three times and it will come to you"). Repeating the materials in order to retrieve what has been lost is symbolized by reaching out to the teacher who has been lost. Similarly, the retrieval of the forgotten Torah is symbolized by the renewed presence of the teacher. This demonstrates the close link between what the student learns and his sense of the teacher's presence. It highlights the central idea of the midrash's earlier sections: when students experience their teacher to be fundamentally disconnected from the relational dimensions of the triangular interactions, not only is the teacher not fulfilling his instrumental role (e.g., to mediate the subject matter for the student's learning), but he is failing to immerse himself in the essential union between the instructional and the interpersonal dimensions of teaching. It is from this perspective that the midrash insists on paths that lead to repair, as well as on the student's and the community's responsibilities to engage in those processes.

Relationships for Learning: Contemporary Resonances

This midrash reflects a refined awareness of relationships and particularly of disrupted relationships in learning. Relationships have become an important focus of contemporary educational discourse. Thus, for instance, *relational pedagogy* is defined as an approach to education in which teachers are guided by "an ethic of caring," teach to the holistic needs of students, create relevant learning experiences, and are committed to developing connections with their students.[29] Relational pedagogy treats relationships as the foundation of good teaching, and builds on the strong emphasis on relationships already embedded in pedagogy itself. It is infused by a number of theories that operate on the basis of the idea that learning is essentially a social process, which makes relationships a focus in understanding how students learn. Thus, educational researcher and teacher educator Barbara McCombs writes that good instruction is not enough; caring relationships are necessary as well: "teachers acting as mentors and forming strong relationship with their students are related to improved academic performance."[30] Dorothy Faulkner follows in the footsteps of Lev Vigotzky (1896–1934), the founder of cultural-historical psychology, according to whom mental functioning in the individual can only be understood by paying close attention to the social and cultural processes from which it derives.[31] And Miriam Raider-Roth echoes

---

[29]   Noddings, *Caring*; Nel Noddings, *The Challenge to Care in Schools* (New York: Teachers College Press, 1992). Relational pedagogy is an approach to teaching and learning that evolved out of the feminist movement in the sixties, as a critique of the existing order of institutions and educational systems. Feminist pedagogy is described as "a reformation of the relationship between professor and student, empowerment, building community, privileging voice, respecting diversity of personal experience, and challenging traditional pedagogical notions" (Lynne M. Webb, Myria W. Allen, and Kandi L. Walker, "Feminist Pedagogy: Identifying Basic Principles," *Academic Exchange Quarterly* 6, no. 1 [2002]: 1). For a review of theories of relational psychology that infuse relational pedagogy and approaches to learning, see Raider-Roth, Stieha, and Hensley, "Rupture and Repair"; Raider-Roth and Holzer, "Learning to be Present."

[30]   Barbara L. McCombs, *Learner-Centered Classroom Practices and Assessments: Maximizing Student Motivation, Learning and Achievement* (Thousand Oaks: Corwin Press, 2007), 64. Other educational psychologists discuss the impact of negative as well as positive teacher expectations and interactions on students' academic performance. Theodore Sizer points to lack of personalization: Theodore Sizer, *Horace's Compromise: The Dilemma of the American High School* (New York: Houghton Mifflin Co., 1984). See also Judith Deiro, *Teaching with Heart: Making Healthy Connections with Students* (Thousand Oaks: Corwin Press, 1996); Tom Gregory, "School Reform and the No-Man's-Land of High School Size," *Proceedings of the Journal of Curriculum Theorizing Conference* (2000).

[31]   McCombs, *Learner-Centered Classroom Practices and Assessments*, 27; Dorothy Faulkner, *Learning Relationships in the Classroom* (London: Routledge, 1998).

John Dewey (1859–1952), who understood relationships as the essential foundation for learning because the transaction that occurs between an individual and the social environment is the "bedrock of knowledge and the fundamental way that knowledge is built."[32] Consequently, teachers need to understand their students' abilities, and it is clear that positive or negative learning relationships cause students to connect or to disassociate from certain knowledge.[33] At the same time, other scholars have voiced criticism of what they consider an exaggerated emphasis on relationships, which they believe is a major cause of the deterioration of academic rigor, diminishing the intellectual purpose of schools and ultimately yielding lower academic achievement.[34] Indeed, building relationships without improving student learning does not constitute good pedagogy.[35]

All of this literature addresses teachers, seeking to make them more aware of the central role of relationships. This focus has also yielded practical tools designed to help teachers cultivate

About the impact of teachers' relationships on students' motivation to learn: Judith A. Deiro, *Teaching with Heart: Making Healthy Connections with Students* (Thousand Oaks: Corwin Press, 1996).

[32]   Miriam Raider-Roth, *Trusting What You Know: The High Stakes of Classroom Relationships* (San Francisco: Josey-Bass, 2005), 27.

[33]   John Dewey, *Experience and Education* (Toronto: Collier-Books Canada, 1963). See also Nel Noddings, The Challenge to Care in Schools. Other educational psychologists discuss the impact of negative as well as positive teacher expectations and interactions on the academic performances of students: Jere Brophy and Thomas Good, Teacher-Student Relationships (New York: Holt, Rinehart & Winston, 1974). The emotional aspect implied in "caring" is discussed at length by Nel Noddings: "a state of mental suffering or of engrossment; to care is to be in a burdened mental state, one of anxiety, fear or solicitude about something or someone [. . .] to care may mean to be charged with the protection, welfare, or maintenance of something or someone" (Noddings, Caring, 9).

[34]   Diane Ravitch, *Left Back: A Century of Battles Over School Reform* (New York: Simon & Schuster, 2000); Eric Donald Hirsch, *The Schools We Need and Why We Don't Have Them* (New York: Anchor Books, 1996).

[35]   Ray Boyd, Neil MacNeill, and Greg Sullivan, "Relational Pedagogy: Putting Balance Back into Students' Learning," *Curriculum Leadership* 4, no. 13 (2006): 1–5.

relationships, especially when students disconnect from the lesson for any reason.[36] At the same time, it is important to recognize that relational disconnections are inevitable and expected during classroom teaching, but also offer opportunities for growth, as discussed by Miriam Raider-Roth, Vicky Stieha, and Bill Hensley.[37] They argue for the need for pedagogical initiatives designed to assist *learners* to cope with disruptions in relationships in productive ways. Beyond that which is emphasized in their article, a broader perspective of this literature shows that their conclusion reflects an important change in focus as it shifts the addressing of pedagogical concerns about relationships from the teachers to students: e.g., how might students become more cognizant of ruptures they experience in learning relationships; what may be avenues for repair?

The midrash discussed in this chapter can serve as grist for the mill to articulate a number of reflections for further investigation in the context of contemporary education. First, at a practical-pedagogical level, the midrash empowers students with awareness, guiding them to the realization that they are responsible for naming their experienced ruptures in the learning triangle and for undertaking action toward repair. This calls for teachers to develop pedagogical means to reach such goals, in keeping with students' ages and levels of maturity. How might students learn to identify and recognize disruptions that are likely to occur in learning? How could students learn to articulate such perceived disruptions and initiate their repair? The midrash challenges the contemporary

---

[36]   Dawn Skorczewski, *Teaching One Moment at a Time: Disruption and Repair in the Classroom* (Amherst: University of Massachusetts Press, 2005).

[37]   Raider-Roth, Stieha, and Hensley, "Rupture and Repair"; Carole Gilligan, *Joining the Resistance* (Cambridge, UK: Polity Press, 2011); Judith V. Jordan, "Relational Resilience," in *The Complexity of Connection: Writings from the Stone Center's Jean Baker Miller Training Institute*, ed. Judith V. Jordan, Maureen Walker, and Lisa M. Hartling (New York: Guilford Press, 2004), 28–46. Raider-Roth, *Trusting What You Know*; Edward Z. Tronick and Kathrine M. Weinberg, "Depressed Mothers and Infants: Failure to Form Dyadic States of Consciousness," in *Postpartum Depression and Child Development*, ed. Lynne Murray and Peter Cooper (New York: Guilford Press, 1997), 54–84.

educator to ask what it would take to evoke such awareness and to offer practicable options for students who experience a teacher as failing in the very basic relationships that are expected of him. What would it take to cultivate students' sense of caring for their own learning in a responsible way, without putting the teacher completely at the mercy of students' potential caprices or of any lack of personal "chemistry" between them? How might students' complaints about teachers in regard to those essential learning relationships be channeled to offer avenues of repair and growth?

From a philosophical perspective, the midrash elicits questions that are worth considering as well. First, in a market-driven society, which views of moral accountability might undergird teachers' work, and how do these views interact with students' perceptions of teachers' responsibility? Second, in linking students' impediments to studying the subject matter with a concern for future (moral) conduct, the midrash reflects a view of teaching that is not confined to academic achievement but rather seeks to operate with a vision of cultivating a full person. Is there still room for this type of view in contemporary education? If so, on what basis? If not, what might it tell us about the ways we think about teachers, students, relationships, and learning?

Chapter Seven

THE VISAGES OF LEARNING INTERACTIONS[1]

And your eyes shall see your teachers.[2]
                                        —*Isaiah*

The Torah has seventy visages.[3]

Your face, my thane, is as a book where people may
read strange matters.[4]
                                        —*William Shakespeare*

It is hard to decide whether what affected us
more and was of greater importance to us was our
concern with the sciences that we were taught or
with the personalities of our teachers.[5]
                                        —*Sigmund Freud*

Introduction

The human visage is a constant object of fascination. From early
infancy, human beings react to facial expressions. The visage is

---

[1] *The Merriam-Webster Dictionary* defines "visage" as a person's face,
    countenance, or appearance. In this chapter, I alternate between "face" and
    "visage." See also Susan Handelman, "'Knowledge Has a Face': The Jewish,
    the Personal, and the Pedagogical," in *Personal Effects: The Social Character of
    Scholarly Writing*, ed. Deborah Holdstein and David Bleich (Logan, UT: Utah
    State University Press, 2001), 121–144.

[2] Isaiah 30:20.

[3] Bamidbar Rabba 13:15–16; Abraham Ibn Ezra, *Introduction to Torah
    Commentary*; Nachmanides on *Genesis* 8:4.

[4] William Shakespeare, *Macbeth*, Act I, Scene 5.

[5] Sigmund Freud, "Some Reflections on Schoolboy Psychology," in *The Standard
    Edition of the Complete Psychological Works of Sigmund Freud: Volume 20*, ed. and
    trans. James Strachey (London: Hogarth, 1914), 242.

the foundation of all social communication and at the same time is the source of unconscious prejudices. The most expressive part of the body, the face attracts the most attention in verbal and nonverbal interactions. A strong instrumental impetus has driven cognitive psychologists and a variety of other scientists to delve into investigations of facial expressions, which bear importance in many realms.[6] The businessman learns how to read cues in the visage of the person with whom he is negotiating. The poker player may gain an advantage over fellow players who do not have good "poker faces." Teachers may better manage classroom dynamics if they tune in to students' facial expressions. In contrast to these instrumental orientations, philosophers reflect on the experience of the human visage as a major window into their philosophies of existence.[7] In 1923, Martin Buber published his famous essay, "I and Thou," on the dialogical principle of existence. Two years later, in an address at an educational conference in Heidelberg, he applied his dialogical concept to the teacher-student relationship, describing an instance of a teacher's interface with students:

> He enters the school-room for the first time, he sees them crouching at the desks, indiscriminately flung together, the misshapen and the well-proportioned, animal faces, empty faces, and noble faces in indiscriminate confusion, like the presence of the created universe; the glance of the educator accepts and receives them all.[8]
>
> But then his eyes meet a face which strikes him. It is not a beautiful face nor particularly intelligent; but it is a real face, or rather, the chaos preceding the cosmos of a real face. On it he reads a question which is something different from the general curiosity: "Who are you? Do you know something that concerns

---

6   Paul Ekman, "Facial Expressions," in *Handbook of Cognition and Emotion,* ed. Tim Dalgleish and Mick Power (West Sussex, England: John Wiley and Sons Ltd., 1999), 301–320.

7   Max Picard, *The Human Face,* trans. Guy Endore (New York: Farrar & Rinehart, 1930); Emmanuel Levinas, *Totality and Infinity: An Essay on Exteriority,* trans. Alphonso Lingis (Dordrecht, The Netherlands: Kluwer Academic Publishers, 1991).

8   Buber, *Between Man and Man,* 112.

me? Do you bring me something? What do you bring?" In some
way he reads the question. And he, the young teacher, addresses
this face. He says nothing very ponderous or important, he puts
an ordinary introductory question: "What did you talk about last
in geography?"[9]

Buber gives voice to an inner, silent conversation, the teacher's
nonverbal communication with his students' visages. In doing so,
he uncovers an aspect of attuned learning in the form of teachers'
and students' reciprocal readings of, and responses to, the face,
which acts as an anchor of their interactions. Emmanuel Levinas
describes how the student's encounter with the subject matter
is mediated through its very concrete manifestation within the
teacher's physical presence, facial expression, and voice. Thus, for
Levinas, a student's openness toward what is being taught cannot
be separated from the welcoming manner of the teacher:

> Ideas instruct me coming from the master who presents them
> to me: who puts them in question; the objectification and
> theme upon which objective knowledge opens already rest on
> teaching. The calling into question of things in a dialectic is not
> a modifying of the perception of them; it coincides with their
> objectification. The object is presented when we have *welcomed*
> an interlocutor. The master, the coinciding of the teaching and
> the teacher, is not in turn a fact among others. The present of the
> manifestation of the master who teaches overcomes the anarchy
> of facts.[10]

---

9   Ibid., 133–134.

10   Emmanuel Levinas, *Totality and Infinity: An Essay on Exteriority*, 69–70 (my
     emphasis). See also: "Attention is attention to something because it is attention
     to someone. The exteriority of its point of departure is essential to it: it is
     the very tension of the I. The school, without which no thought is explicit,
     conditions science. It is there that is affirmed the exteriority that accomplishes
     freedom and does not offend it: the exteriority of the Master. Thought can
     become explicit only among two; explication is not limited to finding what
     one already possessed. But the first teaching of the teacher is his very presence
     as teacher from which representation comes" (Ibid., 99–100). Martin Buber
     has similar ideas as it comes to the teacher's educational impact on the
     student, as will further be discussed in the last section of this chapter. See for
     example: "Only in his whole being, in all his spontaneity can the educator

The image of the human face has served for millennia in Western culture as a primary and primordial opening between the human and the divine. Scholars have also commented on the dynamic and elusive character of the human visage. The Hebrew word *panim* ("face," or "visage") is a plural noun, which may allude to the range of thoughts and emotions it expresses and conceals. In addition, by changing the vowels, which are secondary to consonants in Hebrew, the word becomes *p'nim* ("inwardness," or the "inside"). Yaakov Tzvi Mecklenburg (1785–1865), the German rabbi and scholar best known as the author of the Torah commentary *Haktav Vehakabbalah*, writes that the similarity of *panim* and *p'nim* reflects the intertwinement of the external and the internal, the seen and the concealed.[11] *Panim* also carries a relational meaning: its root consonants *(peh, nun, heh*—which can transform into a *yud* or a *tav)* can also form the verb *lifnot el*—"to turn toward," "to face," or, in a broader sense, "to address." This chapter discusses the use of *panim* in three rabbinic expressions with regard to teacher and student interactions:[12] *lir'ot/lehar'ot panim* (to see/to show the visage), *lehasbir panim* (literally, to explain the visage, but also to illuminate it), and *lekabel panim* (to welcome and to receive the visage). The analysis will show how these expressions sensitize teachers

---

truly affect the whole being of his pupil. For educating characters you do not need a moral genius, but you do need a man who is wholly alive and able to communicate himself directly to his fellow beings. His aliveness streams out to them and affects them most strongly and purely when he has no thought of affecting them" (Buber, *Between Man and Man*, 134).

[11]   Yaakov Tzvi Mecklenburg, *Sefer Haktav VehaKabbalah Vol 2* (New York: Friedman Press, 1971), 20.

והנה לפי המבואר למעיין בזה העניין שכחות הנפשיות מתגלות ביותר על פרצוף הפנים, יתכן לפי זה מאד שם פנים בלשוננו, כי מהוראתו דבר והפוכו יורה על שטח החיצון הנגלה והנראה כמו "להצהיל פנים משמן", וכן יורה על התוך והפנימי, כמו "כל כבודה בת מלך פנימה".

I thank Moshe Sokolow for referring me to this source.

[12]   It is worth reminding the reader that face-to-face oral interchange is a central learning format of early rabbinic teaching, involving memorization, recitation, comparison, and critical analysis of memorized texts. See Martin S. Jaffee, "A Rabbinic Ontology of the Written and Spoken Word: On Discipleship, Transformative Knowledge, and the Living Texts of Oral Torah," *Journal of the American Academy of Religion* 65, no. 3 (1996): 537.

and learners to a subtle extra-verbal, spiritual, and physically embedded dimension of teaching and learning that provides the seeds for a critical reflection on contemporary widespread beliefs and assumptions about teaching.

To See the Face

Rava was a charismatic teacher who attracted many students to his academy.[13] One of his most distinguished students, Rabbi Mesharshya (fourth century, Babylon), offers two notable pieces of advice:

> Rabbi Mesharshya said to his sons: "When you wish to go learn before your teacher, first study the words of the Mishna well, and only then come before your teacher. And when you sit before your teacher, look at your teacher's mouth. As it says: 'but your eyes will watch your guide.'"[14]

The first instruction seems to be a straightforward matter of being prepared for class; however, Rashi adds that familiarizing oneself with a text in advance enables students to ask pertinent questions.[15] The quote from Isaiah 30:20 in support of the second piece of advice refers to looking to *morecha*, translated here as "your guide."[16] In rabbinic literature, however, the word *moreh* connotes "teachers," and Isaiah's injunction usually is understood as the importance of learning from a teacher's behavior. This reflects the view that Torah is a way of life, and thus can be learned from the sages' behavior.

---

13   See Chapter Five, Footnote 21.

14   Talmud, Tractate Kritut 6a

רב משרשיא לבניה כי בעיתו למיזל למגמר קמיה רבכון גרוסו מעיקרא מתני' והדר עולו קמי רבכון וכי יתביתו קמי רבכון חזו לפומיה דרבכון שנאמר (ישעיהו ל) והיו עיניך רואות את מוריך.

15   Rashi in Talmud, Tractate Horayot 12a.

16   NJPS translation;

ונתו לכם אדני לחם צר ומים לחץ ולא יכנף עוד. כי עם בציון ישב בירושלם בכו לא תבכה חנון יחנך לקול זעקך כשמעתו ענך מוריך והיו עיניך רואות את מוריך.

In face-to-face conversation as well as in class, at least in some cultures, individuals tend to look at the visage and especially the eyes. In contrast, Rabbi Mesharshya advises his sons to focus on the teacher's mouth. Is this just a technique for improving attention, hearing, and comprehension? While it is possible to interpret this text instrumentally, from a phenomenological perspective, it also invites a more philosophical interpretation. Rather than interpreting these as two separate pieces of advice, linking the two yields another insight: being familiar with the texts enables a student to look up from the page and focus on the teacher's mouth. The threshold between internal and external, the mouth is simultaneously a concrete part of the teacher's body and a symbolic location where the Torah comes alive audibly. Words are more than cognitive references to abstract knowledge; words and the ideas they convey reach those who listen by being embedded first in the teacher's physical body, her mouth, her voice, her intonation, and in the emotional dimension of her voice. In cultures of oral learning, the transmission of wisdom cannot be separated from extra-cognitive, personal, individualized dimensions of tradition.[17]

To Illuminate the Face

Light is a universal symbol with positive connotations: spirituality, knowledge, life, the divine. Plato's myth of leaving the cave to find the sun's light reflects Greek and Western culture's symbolic use of light for rational understanding. Such is the etymological origin of the verb *to clarify*, as well as the Enlightenment's use in reference

---

[17] Such a conceptual idea is developed in the works of late Hasidic masters. For example, Rabbi Zadok Hacohen Rabinowitz of Lublin (1823–1900), comments on the first mishna of the Ethics of the Fathers: "Moses received the Torah from Sinai and transmitted it to Joshua. Joshua transmitted it to the ancients, and the ancients to the prophets etc." For Rabbi Zadok, this text conveys the real meaning of transmission by emphasizing that Torah is transmitted by and through concrete human beings. Zadok Hacohen of Lublin, *Resisei Layla* (Bnei Brak: Yachhut Press, 1967), 160–161.

to the era of reason.[18] The Book of Ecclesiastes expresses a similar metaphor, but rather than locating the light outside the person, it emphasizes the physical effect of the shining face:

> Who is as the wise man? And who knows the interpretation of a thing? A man's wisdom makes his face shine, and the boldness of his face is changed.[19]

This specific interlacing of wisdom and its expression in the face is a pattern in rabbinic literature. Thus the Talmud tells a story about Rabbi Abahu, a sage who studied at the academy headed by Rabbi Yochanan in Tiberias in the third century:

> Rabbi Abahu came to Tiberias. Rabbi Yochanan's students saw him with his face lit up. They said before Rabbi Yochanan: "Rabbi Abahu has found a treasure." [Rabbi Yochanan] said to them: "Why do you think so?" They said to him: "His face lit up." He said to them: "Perhaps he has heard a new lesson [or "word of Torah"]." When Rabbi Abahu came before [Rabbi Yochanan], [Rabbi Yochanan] said to him: "What new lesson have you heard?" [Rabbi Abahu] said to him: "An old supplementary teaching." Rabbi Yochanan applied to him: "A person's wisdom lights up his face." (Ecclesiastes 8:1)[20]

This short story counters two popular perceptions. The students believe that the shining face reflects a person's financial gain, but their wise teacher knows that it also could reflect the acquisition of new knowledge. This perception is then further refined, since Rabbi Abahu has not learned a new lesson *per se* but a *tosefta atika*—an ancient, small portion of legal knowledge that can serve as a key to the understanding of other legal passages.

While texts such as this one attune the reader to people's shining faces as an involuntary outcome of learning experiences, the rabbinic expression *lehasbir panim* ("to explain," "to clarify the visage") is used in reference to an intentional engagement on the

---

18   Etymologically, *clarity* comes from the Latin "claritas," indicating brightness, thus related to light.

19   Ecclesiastes 8:1. מי כהחכם ומי יודע פשר דבר חכמת אדם תאיר פניו ועז פניו ישנא

20   Jerusalem Talmud, Tractate Pesachim 69a.

part of the teacher. To appreciate the radical idea conveyed in the following rabbinic source, it is necessary first to pay attention to the biblical source that uses the word *panim* (face) in divine-human relationships, specifically God's revelation at Sinai:

> The Lord our God made a covenant with us in Chorev. The Lord made not this covenant with our fathers, but with us, even us, who are all of us here alive this day. The Lord spoke with you *face to face* in the mount out of the midst of the fire.[21]

The term "face to face" evokes directness, closeness, and personal address; perhaps even intimacy. The Talmud applies it to the interface of learning and teaching, and for that purpose turns God into a co-learner, revealed to Moses in the Tent of Meeting.

> "And the Lord spoke unto Moses face to face." (Exodus 33:11) Rabbi Yitzchak said: "the Holy One, blessed be He, said to Moses: Moses, I and thou will propound views on the halacha" [*nasbir panim behalacha*, literally, "we shall clarify faces in halacha"].[22]

According to Rabbi Yitzchak, God invites Moses to a joint study of the legal elements of the Torah. The term *lehasbir panim* refers directly to explaining and clarifying the subject matter, and yet it also contains the word for visages, the faces of halacha that are waiting to be illuminated. This text predates the medieval rabbinic concept of "the seventy faces of Torah," a symbolic number indicating the numerous interpretations and meanings that are embedded in the Torah.[23] Even revealed by God, religious law is not a sealed body

---

21   Deuteronomy 5:2–4.

יהוה אלוהינו, כרת עימנו ברית–בחורב. לא את-אבותינו, כרת יהוה את-הברית הזאת: כי איתנו, אנחנו אלה
פה היום כולנו חיים. פנים בפנים, דיבר יהוה עימכם בהר–מתוך האש.

22   Talmud, Tractate Brachot 63b.

ודבר ה' אל משה פנים אל פנים. אמר ר' יצחק אמר לו הקב"ה למשה: משה אני ואת נסביר פנים בהלכה.
איכא דאמרי כך אמר לו הקב"ה למשה, כשם שאני הסברתי לך פנים, כך אתה הסבר פנים לישראל והחזר
האוהל למקומו.

23   Midrash Bamidbar Rabba, 13:15–16; Abraham Ibn Ezra, *Introduction to Torah Commentary*; Nachmanides on Genesis 8:4. See Chananel Mack, "The Seventy Faces of Torah: On the Genealogy of an Idiom," in *Jubilee Book in the Honor of Rabbi Mordechai Breuer: Articles in Jewish Studies Vol. 2*, ed. Moshe Bar-Asher (Jerusalem: Akademon Press, 1992), 449–462.

of knowledge; it requires study, clarification, and illumination of what the law actually entails and implies, beyond the confines of the revealed words—past the *panim*, the meeting point of the visible and the concealed.[24]

In a similar vein, Rabbi Elazar of Modiin (a disciple of Rabbi Yohanan, the son of Zakkai, and an expert on homiletics, first and second centuries, Israel) says that an individual who interprets the Torah contrary to its true intent (*hamegaleh panim baTorah shelo kehalacha*), although he may possess Torah knowledge and good deeds, has no share in the World to Come.[25] The expression *hamegaleh panim batorah shelo kehalacha* (literally, "uncovers faces of the Torah through inappropriate methods," or "uncovers inappropriate faces in the Torah") establishes normative limits on interpretations or disrespectful attitudes toward the Torah.[26] In the present context, the word *panim* refers to the meaning or implications that draw on, but are not limited to, the written word. Like the human face, which expresses both the concretely tangible and the amorphously sensed (i.e., emotions), the Torah allows for similar interplay.

Another rabbinic text likens the human visage's range of emotional expressions to various genres of Torah literature, personifying each as projecting a particular mood:

> "Face(s) to face(s) did the Lord speak with you" (Deuteronomy 5:4): "Faces"—two; "to faces"—two; four faces altogether: an

---

[24] In Talmud, Tractate Sanhedrin 93b, Rashi explains "to show faces in halacha" as the bringing of a rationale, a legal basis or precedent that sustains the law. Thus again, the word *panim* is used to refer to something beyond that which is perceived on the surface.

[25] *Ethics of the Fathers* 3:11.

ר' אלעזר המודעי אומר . . . והמגלה פנים בתורה שלא כהלכה, אף על פי שיש בידו תורה ומעשים טובים אין לו חלק לעולם הבא.

About R. Elazar, see Talmud, Baba Batra 10b.

[26] Talmud, Tractate Sanhedrin 99b, in reference to King Menashe, who extracted erroneous conclusions from Torah; Jerusalem Talmud, Tractate Peah 5a uses the term in reference to someone who denies the divine origin of the Torah. Maharal uses the term to indicate denigration of either the Torah or its sages, see Maharal, "Netiv Hatorah," in *Netivot Olam* (Jerusalem: Sifrei Yehadut Pub., 1971), 50–53.

awesome face for Scripture; an ordinary face for Mishna; a smiling
face for Talmud; an ingratiating face for aggadah.[27]

By personifying each type of Torah literature as projecting a
particular mood, the text emphasizes the affective aspects that
arise during its study. Finally, *lehasbir panim* also means putting
on a cheerful face. In discussing the meaning of the "face-to-face"
interaction that took place between God and Moses in the Tent of
Meeting (Exodus 33:11), the second part of the midrash says:

> "And the Lord spoke unto Moses face to face" [. . .] Some say that
> the Holy One, blessed be He, said thus to Moses: Just as I have
> turned upon you a cheerful face [*hesbarti lecha panim*], so do you
> turn upon Israel a cheerful face [*hasber panim*] and restore the tent
> to its place. And he would return to the camp.[28]

Here, *lehasbir panim* does not explicitly refer to the subject
matter. While in the first part of the midrash, God invites Moses to
engage jointly in the illumination of the face of halacha, in this part,
lehasbir panim refers to the interpersonal realm between God (here
in the role of teacher) and Moses (the student who then becomes
the teacher). The idiom emphasizes the importance of the teacher's
cheerful face, something Moses is to emulate when teaching
Torah to the Israelites. This midrash is designed to heighten the
teacher's consciousness of the impact of his visage on students. The

---

[27]   Talmud, Tractate Soferim 16b.

אמרו פנים בפנים דבר ה' הא ד' הא ד' אפין, פנים של אימה למקרא, פנים בינוניות למשנה, פנים מסבירות לש"ס,
פנים שוחקות לאגדה.

See also Psikta Chapter 21:10.

[28]   Talmud, Tractate Brachot 63b.

ודבר ה' אל משה פנים אל פנים וכו' [איכא דאמרי כך אמר לו הקב"ה למשה כשם שאני הסברתי לך פנים, כך
אתה הסבר פנים לישראל והחזר האוהל למקומו.

The returning of the tent refers to Exodus 33:7–11 in which, following God's
revelation to him, Moses moves the Tent of Meeting outside the Israelite
camp. In this tent, God speaks to Moses "face to face": "Then the Lord would
speak to Moses face to face, as a man would speak to his companion, and
he would return to the camp" (Exodus 33:11). The sages interpret the words
"and he would return to the camp" as God's injunction to Moses to return the
tent to the camp.

juxtaposition of the two meanings of *lehasbir panim* in the midrash alludes to subtle connections between the impact of the teacher's face on the student, and aspects of the subject matter the student may experience as enlightening.

To Welcome the Face

According to the Talmud, it is customary for an individual to go and greet his teacher during the festivals.[29] Although the individual is to *set out* to visit his teacher, the idiomatic verb that is used is "to *welcome* the teacher's face"—*lehakbil/lekabel p'nei rabbo*.[30] From a phenomenological perspective, this expression conveys a proactive mode of welcoming, an openness to being affected by the teacher's physical presence—specifically, his visage. As in the earlier examples, this expression raises awareness of the felt, almost tangible impact of the teacher's face. *Lekabel p'nei rabbo* evokes the external/internal, visible/concealed experience of the teacher-student encounter. This idea is further emphasized in rabbinic texts that compare the student's welcoming of the teacher's face to welcoming the "face" of the *Shechina:*

> One who welcomes his teacher [*mekabel p'nei rabbo*, literally: receives his teacher's face], it is as if he is welcoming the *Shechina* [*mekabel p'nei Shechina*, literally: receives the *Shechina*'s face].[31]

In Chapter Four, *Shechina* indicates God's immanent presence in the world, and particularly in human relationships.[32] Transcendence

---

29 Talmud, Tractate Rosh Hashana 16b.

30 Rabbinic sources alternatively use two forms of welcoming, literally "receiving": "*lekabel*" and "*lehakbil*." The root *kuf-bet-lamed* means "in front of," thus "*lehakbil*" means "to come toward a person with the goal of welcoming him," i.e., "*lekabel*."

31 Jerusalem Talmud, Tractate Eruvin, 31a. שכל המקבל פני רבו כאילו מקבל פני שכינה. Rabbinic literature uses similar terms in reference to the welcoming of a friend: Tractate Eruvin, 31a and Mechilta Rabbi Ishmael, Yitro, "Treaty of Amalek," Chapter 1. Also in reference to an elderly person: Yalkut Shimoni, Shmuel, 247:96.

32 Chapter Four, Footnote 27.

lies within the interpersonal interaction between teacher and student. From an experiential, phenomenological perspective, the visage has two dimensions: the external-perceptible and the invisible-internal, which are reflected in the words *panim* (face) and *p'nim* (interior). The seeming connection established between the interpersonal and the more theological discourse underscores the spiritual dimension of the teacher-student relationship. It heightens awareness of the extra-verbal dimension that lies at the heart of the following Talmudic story, which is predicated on the biblical obligation of male Jews to visit the Temple in Jerusalem three times a year. Exodus 23:17 says, "Three times in the year shall all your males appear before the Lord God, the God of Israel."[33]

The Bible uses the word *re'iya*, rendered here as "to appear," but whose basic root literally means "to see," or "to be seen."[34] The rabbinic codification of this obligation appears in the Mishna: "All are bound to appear [can also be read as "all are bound by seeing"] [at the Temple] except a deaf man, etc."[35] *Re'iya* emphasizes the pilgrim's visual experience: to see and to be seen. In the midst of a legalistic discussion of the pilgrimage, the Talmud brings a story involving two characters: Rabbi Yehuda Hanassi* (third century, Israel), known commonly as "Rebbi," who belonged to a dynasty of leading sages and is identified as the editor of the Mishna; and Rabbi Hiyya, another leading sage of Rebbi's time.[36]

---

[33]   Exodus 23:17. שָׁלֹשׁ פְּעָמִים בַּשָּׁנָה יֵרָאֶה כָּל-זְכוּרְךָ. See also 34:23; Deuteronomy16:16.

[34]   ה.א.ה, and in this context יראה, "will be seen."

[35]   Mishna, Tractate Chagiga 1:1; הכל חייבין בראייה חוץ מחרש שוטה וקטן וכו' The Sages debate whether this refers to the actual pilgrimage to the Temple or to the sacrifice called *olat re'iyah*, the "offering of the seen/seeing." The sages differ in their understanding of the modalities of this ritual. For Rabbi Yochanan, it is a matter of "seeing the face of the divine in the Temple's inner courtyard, an unmediated experience of the pilgrim. For Resh Lakish this refers to the seeing of the face when bringing the sacrifice, thus reflecting a feeling of submission.

[36]   Both are also recorded to have deep disagreements on public policy, but it is Rebbi's authority that usually prevailed. See for example, Talmud, Moed Katan 16b.

Rebbi and Rabbi Hiyya were once going on a journey. When they came to a certain town, they said: "if there is a rabbinical scholar here, we shall go and pay him our respects" [literally "receive his face"].[37] They were told: "There is a rabbinical sage here and he is blind" [euphemistically referred to by the expression *meor eynayim*, literally: "eye light"]. Said Rabbi Hiyya to Rebbi: "Stay [here], you must not lower you princely dignity, I shall go and visit him" [*veakbil apeih*—literally, "and I will receive his face"].[38] But [Rebbi] took hold of him and went with him. When they were taking leave from him, he said to them: "You have visited [*hikbaltem panim*, literally: "you have received the face of"] one who is seen but does not see; may you be granted to visit Him [*lehakbil panim*, literally: to receive the face] of the One who sees but is not seen." Said [Rebbi to Rabbi Hiyya]: "If I had listened to you, you would have deprived me of this blessing."[39]

There are many Talmudic stories about sages who visit each other or who happen to meet. These stories teach lessons based on the sages' words or deeds. In this legend, however, the two visitors are about to part. Moreover, the rabbinic scholar remains anonymous, which creates the literary effect of emphasizing his presence/non-presence, a symbolic reflection of the visible/concealed character of the face. Through parallel language, the text establishes an inherent link between the welcoming of the face as a way of relating to one's teacher and an experience of revelation. Going back to the earlier teaching, the parallel drawn between the welcoming of the teacher's and the *Shechina*'s faces alludes to a relationship between the ethical and the metaphysical: "One who welcomes his teacher, *it is as if he is* welcoming the *Shechina*."[40]

---

37 וניקביל אפיה

38 ואקביל אפיה

39 Talmud, Tractate Chagiga 5b.
רבי ורבי חייא הוו שקלי ואזלי באורחא כי מטו לההוא מתא אמרי איכא צורבא מרבנן הכא נזיל וניקביל אפיה אמרי איכא צורבא מרבנן הכא ומאור עינים הוא אמר ליה רבי חייא לרבי תיב את לא תזלזל בנשיאותך איזיל אנא ואקביל אפיה תקפיה ואזל בהדיה כי הוו מיפטרי מיניה אמר להו אתם הקבלתם פנים הנראים ואינן רואין תזכו להקביל פנים הרואים ואינן נראין אמר ליה איכו השתא מנעתן מהאי בירכתא.

40 Jerusalem Talmud, Tractate Eruvin 31a. שכל המקבל פני רבו כאילו מקבל פני שכינה.

The blindness of the scholar creates asymmetry in the relationship. He offers his face to the visitors but cannot see theirs, which may reflect the nonreciprocal nature of teaching: that of giving without necessarily receiving in return.

Another aspect of teaching is represented by the teacher's blindness, which symbolizes the paradoxical nature of his presence/absence relative to the student. If the teacher's seeing can also stand for a means of control, his blindness opens a space that allows the student to develop a distinctive identity.

To Receive the Visage

Rabbi Nachman of Breslov (1772–1810) was the founder of the Breslov Hasidic* sect and among the most creative thinkers of the entire Hasidic movement.[41] A great-grandson of the Baal Shem Tov, who founded Hasidism, Rabbi Nachman—ironically—rejected the idea of hereditary Hasidic dynasties. Instead, he believed that each Hasid must "search for the righteous person for himself and within himself." His teachings reflect intra- and inter-psychological intuitions, both in the realm of Torah study and with regard to the teacher-student relationship.

Rabbi Nachman offers a new interpretation of the student's "receiving" of the teacher's visage (*kabbalat p'nei rabbo*). He begins by using the rabbinic metaphor that compares Moses' relationship to Joshua, his disciple, with the relationship between the sun, which radiates its own light, and the moon, whose light is a reflection of the sun's. But, he adds, if the moon were to be corporeal, dense, and dark, or unpolished, it would not be able to receive the light of the sun at all. In parallel,

> If the student has a *panim*—i.e., the aspect of "shining *panim*," [like] a polished mirror—he can then "receive the *panim*," receive the light of the *panim* of the teacher. At that point, the teacher

---

41   Arthur Green, *Tormented Master: The Life and Spiritual Quest of Rabbi Nahman of Bratslav* (Woodstock: Jewish Lights Publishing, 1992); Tzvi Mark, *Revelation and Repair in the Explicit and Esoteric Writings of Rabbi Nachman of Bratslav* (Jerusalem: Magnes Press, 2011).

should be able to observe himself [reflected] in the *panim* of the
student who receives his *panim*. This is like with any polished
mirror, anyone who stands facing it sees himself in the mirror. It
has to be that way here as well. The student should "receive the
panim" of the teacher—he should absorb the *panim* of the teacher
within himself—so that the *panim* of the teacher can be observed
in him. This is the meaning of *kabbalat panim*, actually receiving
the *panim*. Yet, this is specifically if the student has a *panim*—i.e.,
"shining *panim*," corresponding to a polished mirror, as above.
But if he has no *panim*—i.e., he is an aspect of "dark *panim*"—
then he is unable to "receive the *panim*" in the manner mentioned
above regarding the sun and the moon. The *panim* of the teacher
can certainly not be observed in him, as when one stands facing
something thick and dark.[42]

This deep meaning of "receiving his teacher's face" stands in
contrast to a student who shows a "dark *panim*" (which literally
would mean "has no face"), meaning that it does not reflect the
teacher's shining face. Is Rabbi Nachman implying that a teacher
has a narcissistic need to see the student molded in his own image?
The uniquely intense, semi-private, and often personal relationships
between Hasidic masters and their disciples serve as a referential
context of Rabbi Nachman's teachings, as he explains.[43] Rabbi
Nachman connects the "dark *panim*" to a focus on the material,[44]
which indicates a fundamental way of relating to others, to life,
and to knowledge. This echoes Erich Fromm's distinction between
having and being as "two fundamental modes of experience, the
respective strengths of which determine the differences between
the characters of individuals and various types of social character."[45]

---

[42] Nachman of Breslov, *Likutey Moharan* (Jerusalem: Breslov Research Institute,
1990), 234–238.

[43] Joseph Weiss, "Torah Study in Early Hasidism," in *Studies in Eastern European
Mysticism*, ed. David Goldstein (Oxford: Littman Library, 1985), 56–68; Tali
Loewenthal, "Early Hasidic Teachings—Esoteric Mysticism, or a Medium of
Communal Leadership?," *Journal of Jewish Studies* 37 (1986): 58–75.

[44] *Ta'avat mammon*. This is a theme that runs throughout his teachings. See, for
example, *Likutey Moharan*, Chapters 13, 23, 30, and 230.

[45] Erich Fromm, *To Have or To Be?* (New York: Continuum, 2008), 14.

A student's "dark face" is a metaphor for a possessive attitude toward the Torah that is taught, perhaps coupled with its being perceived as consisting of nothing greater than objective data to be mastered.

Rabbi Nachman contrasts this attitude to the student's openness to be touched and moved by the unspoken dimension of teaching — of the living Torah that is imbued with and embedded within the teacher's shining visage. This text does not discuss whether or how the teacher might help the student cultivate such a "receptive face," but it does seek to attune the teacher to this dimension of teaching, further echoed in spiritual traditions of dialogue.[46] It highlights the existential dimension of learning, pointing to a unique feature of the teacher-student relationship in which the student does not *a priori* resist self-transformation.[47] Rabbi Nachman extends this idea back to God's revelation: "*panim bepanim* [face to face] God spoke with you."[48] Rabbi Nachman interprets "*panim bepanim*" as indicating that the Israelites were in a "shining visage" mode:

> They were able to "receive the *panim*" of holiness, i.e., the *panim* of holiness was observable in them. This is the meaning of "*panim bepanim*." The *panim* of holiness was in their visages.... And thus, "God spoke with you."[49]

The term *holiness* in this context refers to a spiritual dimension that transcends a human being's natural, predetermined physical constitution. Openness to the transcendent dimension of existence requires receptiveness. This is echoed whenever the teacher's face is welcomed by a student, leading to an existential change, the sense of a vivid presence in the student, which on the one hand

---

[46] See for example, Buber, *Between Man and Man.*

[47] Thus I would not reduce Rabbi Nachman's teaching to the teacher's hope to see the student thinking precisely the same way as the teacher. The idea of the teacher's face being present in that of the student does not imply similar intellectual content but reflects an extra-verbal dimension of their relationship.

[48] Deuteronomy 5:4.

[49] Deuteronomy 5:5.

is perceived in the countenance of his face but at the same time remains amorphous and inarticulable.

Contemporary Resonances

Our lives are saturated with human faces: on television and electronic screens, at every street corner, and on the digital devices we constantly consult. Our eyes see more visages in one day than people two centuries ago saw over the course of a year. And yet, defining what animates the human face remains a challenge. Even more important is the impact of the mode of our consciousness when we are looking at people's faces and what we are aware of and sensitive to. What happens to teachers and students if and when they consciously open themselves to each other's visages as implied in these texts? In Chapter Six, the midrash is sensitive to the change in countenance when teacher-student relationships are disrupted. The rabbinic texts in this chapter direct students' and teachers' focus to three central dimensions of teaching, which reflect kernels of broader philosophical views that may challenge trends of contemporary educational discourse. They uncover a dimension of extra-verbal effects within learning when it is mediated through the visage. With the exception of Rabbi Nachman, the texts are vague about the nature of these effects, which may reflect the twofold nature of the experience: palpable, on the one hand, and not available for thorough conceptualization because of its elusive nature on the other.[50] These rabbinic texts reflect a dimension of teaching that is

---

[50] This double aspect is reflected in Emmanuel Levinas' analysis of the experience of the face of the Other, which oscillates between failed attempts, conceptualizations, and a phenomenological description of the lived experience. See Emmanuel Levinas, *Totality and Infinity*, 187–219. See also in the philosophical writings of Jan Patočka who makes a principled claim about the nature of philosophical tradition as "a combination of the art of thought and the art of seeing. Philosophy moves between Scylla and Charybdis: between an inability to articulate consistently and precisely what it sees and wants to articulate, and, on the other hand, a precise formalism, keenly honed by tradition and devoid of content" (Jan Patočka, *Body, Community, Language and World* [Chicago: Open Court, 1998], 4). Jan Patočka (1907–1977) is an influential Central European philosopher and phenomenologist

incarnated in, and projected by, the teacher's visage. Teachers do not merely convey disembodied ideas. While educational discourse often emphasizes teachers' cognitive abilities to communicate ideas and concepts, these texts suggest that teachers also color what is taught through their presence, emotions, voices, intonations, and, probably most of all, their visages. Through the visage, teachers infuse the subject matter with a personal vitality and thus subtly individualize the subject matter they teach. The connection that these texts establish with the spiritual realm (e.g., the welcoming of the face of the *Shechina*) alludes to the learner's experience of such felt but undefinable dimensions of learning. The teacher immerses his entire being in making an impact on the learner. These texts reflect teacher-student interactions in cultural contexts that are a far cry from the modern classroom. They contrast sharply with conceptual paradigms of education according to which a teacher's personal emotional impact on the student (and thus also her ties to the subject matter) should be minimized if not neutralized, in order to protect the student's autonomous thinking.[51]

These texts may have a particular *awakening effect* in the era of the digital revolution, especially with increasing voices that suggest replacing face-to-face teaching with distance and screen-centered learning. The spiritual and educational importance of the physical presence, closeness, and face-to-face encounters that these texts point to transcends any narrow pragmatic considerations of such a radical change.[52] These concerns, to be discussed further, lead to

---

of the twentieth century. His works mainly deals with the problem of the original, given world (Lebenswelt), its structure, and the human position and experience of it.

[51] Similar ideas are expressed in the works of modern thinkers as well: Joseph J. Schwab, "Eros and Education: A Discussion of One Aspect of Discussion," in *Science, Curriculum, and Liberal Education: Selected Essays*, ed. Ian Westbury and Neil J. Wilkof (Chicago and London: The University of Chicago Press, 1978), 105–132.

[52] For a discussion in relation to facial expressions, see George Theonas, Dave Hobbs, and Dimitrios Rigas, "The Effect of Facial Expressions on Students in Virtual Educational Environments," *International Scholarly and Scientific Research and Innovation* 1, no. 11 (2007): 334–341; Nicolas C. Burbules, "Navigating the Advantages and Disadvantages of Online Pedagogy," in

questioning and re-examining some views that define teaching as merely helping students access and use information.

Finally, Rabbi Nachman's teaching presents a somewhat judgmental and even top-down or hierarchical view of the teacher-student relationship. Yet, beyond this *prima facie* impression, it may also provide a window into a broader conception of teaching's formative and spiritual aspects that are often excluded from educational discourse.[53] Indeed, Rabbi Nachman's insights invite us to examine potential educative connections among teaching, forms of hierarchical relationships, and student growth.

Learning, Culture and Community in Online Education: Research and Practice, ed. Caroline Haythornthwaite and Michelle M. Kazmer (New York: Peter Lang Publishing, 2004), 3–17.

[53] Herman Hesse, *Magister Ludi: The Glass Bead Game,* trans. Richard Winston and Clara Winston (St. Martin Press, 1943), 223, http://www.starcenter.com/glassbead.pdf: "the pleasure it gives to transplant the achievements of the mind into other minds and see them being transformed into entirely new shapes and emanations"—in other words, the joy of teaching. The second was grappling with the personalities of the students, and the attainment and practice of authority and leadership—in other words, the joy of educating. See also Chapter Eight, the section "Teachers' Attuned Teaching."

Part Four

ATTUNED LEARNING
AND EDUCATIONAL THOUGHT

Chapter Eight

ATTUNED LEARNING IN CONTEMPORARY CONTEXTS

> What to do? How to act? Who to be? These are focal questions for everyone living in circumstances of late modernity—and ones which, on some level or another, all of us answer, either discursively or through day-to-day social behavior.
>
> *—Anthony Giddens* [1]

> Faith is the attitude of one who accepts being interpreted at the same time that he or she interprets the world of the text.
>
> *—Paul Ricoeur* [2]

> At the beginning of the *Republic* Plato tells us that no one can oblige an Other to enter into a discourse.
>
> *—Emmanuel Levinas* [3]

Attuned Learning, Habits of the Heart

A practice-oriented philosophy aims to integrate the fostering of habits of the mind, the hand, and the heart through the learner's practices within the learning dynamic. Thus, a prior book discussed practices that derive from *chavruta* text study as instruments for establishing textual interpretations and conducting dialogues with texts and study partners. However, in a more subtle way, these

---

[1] Anthony Giddens, *Modernity and Self-Identity: Self and Society in the Late Modern Age* (Cambridge: Polity, 1991), 70.

[2] Paul Ricoeur, *Figuring the Sacred: Religion, Narrative and Imagination* (Minneapolis: Fortress Press, 1995), 46.

[3] Emmanuel Levinas, *Difficult Freedom: Essays on Judaism* (Baltimore: The Johns Hopkins University Press, 1997), 178.

practices have also been designed to have formative effects—that is, to help cultivate different perceptions, sensibilities, and ethical dispositions in the learner. At the core of this view is that intentional performance of the practices can more directly cultivate qualities such as sensitivity, listening, wholeheartedness, open-mindedness, vulnerability, responsibility, and an ethical commitment to the partner's learning.[4] In this book, rabbinic literature is utilized as a wellspring for further elaboration of this philosophy. Attuned learning is presented with a similar two-dimensional structure: one that attends to students', teachers', and co-learners' actions and practices, and a second to the more intangible aspects of heightened self-awareness toward others as well as an openness to appearances such as the visage and the transformation of student, subject matter, and teacher. The first attends to habits of the hands. The latter relates to habits of the heart, best described as the marriage between interdependence, emotion, and self-awareness.[5]

While *chavruta* text study practices are initially grounded in habits of the hand, the exploration of attuned learning primarily addresses habits of the heart of co-learners, students, and teachers. Attuned learning resides in what Maxine Green calls a *wide-awakeness* vis-à-vis the mental, emotional, and physical workings of oneself and others. Learning is thus reflected as a psychical event caught in the interplay between what lies outside and inside the person. The modes of engagement in learning are not defined by rules, nor by a set of specific practices. What defines them as attuned cannot be encapsulated by a prescribed list of rule-governed behaviors, ethical codes, or precepts. Rather, attuned learning is a type of understanding that helps discern what is appropriate and important within learning interactions, without needing all of its

---

4   Holzer with Kent, *A Philosophy of Havruta*, 193–207.

5   This definition of habits of the heart is an extension of Lee Shulman's discussion in the context of professional formation, see Lee. S. Shulman, "The Signature Pedagogies of the Professions of Law, Medicine, Engineering, and the Clergy: Potential Lessons for the Education of Teachers" (paper presented at the National Research Council's Center for Education, Irvine, CA, February 6–8, 2005), available at http://www.taylorprograms.org/images/Shulman_Signature_Pedagogies.pdf.

implicit terms to be made explicit. It is a type of understanding that consists of a number of habits such as awareness of one's own and others' vulnerability, genuine openness toward the unexpected, and sensitivity to that which cannot be conceptualized but can be recognized.

Educational Significance of Attuned Learning

As discussed in Chapter One,[6] the word "ethical" is used in a broad sense to include such habits. Rabbinic texts show an attuned person as reflecting an ethical attitude in:

- her sense of responsibility toward another person's learning—that is, the learner's responsibility toward her co-learner's learning (Chapter Four) and the teacher's responsibility toward the student's transformation (Chapter Five);

- her self-awareness regarding her own emotional reactions—such as potential hubris as a co-learner (Chapter Three), subjective reactions to disruptions as a student (Chapter Six), and awareness of one's own transformation as a teacher (Chapter Five);

- her openness to being transformed by the subject matter (Chapter Five) and awareness of the intangible impact of the visage (Chapter Seven).

In light of these, an educational significance of attuned learning is best illustrated in the following story. Years ago, three educators asked me if I could point to a "uniquely Jewish" aspect of learning. To be honest, I find such questions disconcerting. First, I hear a strong, resistant voice bursting from my academic background in Jewish philosophy that says, "There is no way for you to establish what is or isn't uniquely Jewish. Rabbinic culture is comprised of multiple voices, and Judaism is not an island but has been influenced constantly by other cultures and religions." Second, my former self as a student of psychology shows up to ask, "Why do people have a need to believe that they are doing something

---

6   See Chapter One, Footnote 25.

that would be *uniquely Jewish* when they learn?" Nevertheless, in having to address the question, my thoughts would go to specific Jewish works (e.g., the Talmud) whose study could naturally make learning uniquely Jewish. But these educators were asking about a specific attribute in the actual mode of engagement in learning—not in the subject matter. As one educator further clarified, "Are there ways to engage that makes learning a holy activity?"

This clarification only complicates matters, as *holiness* is not an unequivocal term. But, however you understand the term, it always points to the intertwining of habits of the hand with habits of the heart—in this case, a principled concern for a qualitative aspect of learning. Attuned learning thereby provides teachers with an additional educational end worthy of being nurtured, one that relates to learning interactions in the classroom as a locus for the cultivation of habits of the heart.[7] This view of learning has resonances in rabbinic culture, as early rabbinic tradition predicates the acquisition of Torah on the learner's intentional cultivation of dispositions[8] such as listening, comprehension of the heart, awe, fear, humility, joy, serving the sages, companionship with one's contemporaries, debating with one's students, and tranquility.

A second significance of attuned learning is implied in the educator's use of the word "holiness." Rethinking ethical as well as spiritual dimensions of modes of engagement in learning is a high priority, particularly in a society driven by *technical rationality* and *effectiveness*. Emmanuel Levinas' philosophy, which defines ethics as a fundamental openness toward what lies beyond oneself,

7   Building on the work of Martin Buber, Ronald Arnett also indicates the connection between dialogic learning and character-building through conversation. Both the characteristics of the conversation as well as who the partners are become essential to what is learned. See Ronald C. Arnett, *Communication and Community: Implications of Martin Buber's Dialogue* (Carbondale: Southern Illinois University Press, 1986).

8   "Torah is acquired with forty-eight qualities." (*Ethics of the Fathers* 6:6.) The word "acquired" refers not only to the acquisition of Torah knowledge but also to the learner's growth. Dispositions are the expressions of both the heart and the mind: See Linda T. Zagzebski, *Virtues of the Mind: An Inquiry into the Nature of Virtue and the Ethical Foundations of Knowledge* (Cambridge: Cambridge University Press, 1996).

or *transcendence*, as concerning what exists *within* the human experience. He ultimately finds it in ethics: "It is the meaning of the beyond, of transcendence, and not of ethics that our study seeks. It finds this meaning in ethics."[9] In this book, such instances of the ethical intertwining with transcendence have explicitly been applied to Resh Lakish's conceptions of collaborative learning.[10] They have also contributed to the discussion of the visage, a dimension of learning that awakens the reader to inexpressible dimensions of learning interactions.[11] The emphasis on deliberate self-awareness, ethics, and transcendence seems worthy of further exploration as part of a practice-oriented philosophy of education.[12]

---

[9]   See Chapter One, Footnote 25.

[10]   Chapter Four, Footnote 27.

[11]   Chapter Seven, Footnote 28.

[12]   Such exploration is beyond the scope of this book. It would take as its point of departure the "hermeneutic turn"—the growing awareness of the impact of processes of interpretation in literature and philosophy, which emphasizes a refined attention to the ways people engage in meaning-making in general and in the reading of texts in particular. It would further extend to the "theological turn" of phenomenology and hermeneutics, in its aim to reintegrate traditional Jewish religious language in the ways people engage and experience with others, with themselves and, by and large, with concrete instances of life. See Dominique Janicaud, Jean-François Courtine, Jean-Louis Chrétien, Michel Henry, Jean-Luc Marion, and Paul Ricoeur, *Phenomenology and the 'Theological Turn'—The French Debate* (New York: Fordham University Press, 2000). Levinas' philosophy would play a central role in such an endeavor, particularly in his view of ethics as residing in the perception of the Other as an unassimilable and unknowable alterity. It is from such an experience of the ungraspable "otherness of the Other" that moral responsibility occurs. For a discussion of the connection between ethics, religion, and epistemology, for example Richard A. Cohen, "The Face of Truth in Rosenzweig, Levinas, and Jewish Mysticism," in *Phenomenology of the Truth Proper to Religion*, ed. Daniel Guerrière (New York: SUNY Press, 1990), 175–201. Initial theoretical explorations are conducted by Professor Sharon Todd, who challenges a widespread view that learning and *knowing about* the Other (i.e., a person from a different socioeconomic or cultural background) will bring people to treat each other responsibly. Instead, she explores another path for moral education on the basis of the work of Emmanuel Levinas. See Sharon Todd, *Learning From the Other: Levinas, Psychoanalysis, and Ethical Possibilities in Education* (Albany: Sunny Press, 2003), 5. Similarly, educational philosopher Claire Elise Katz discusses Levinas' philosophy as offering a radical

Attuned Learning: Critical Reflections

Bringing ancient texts to bear on contemporary cultural contexts creates tensions that, according to Gadamer, can be utilized for further exploration. This can be particularly helpful assuming, as I believe, that education should not align itself uncritically with its potential social and cultural contexts but rather should call both itself and these cultural environments into critical reflection. The following reflections build on ideas discussed throughout the book.

Co-Learners' Attuned Learning

The metaphor of the two irons emphasizes the value of encountering and arguing with a learning partner's alternative views through uninhibited engagement. While arguing may be central to learning, it also may be at odds with contemporary educational habits and beliefs, from two different—and *a priori* contradictory—perspectives. First, the very idea of arguing with someone else's interpretation of the materials assumes the risk of being labeled not only as "politically incorrect" but as undermining the democratic values of respect for others' opinions. Students often espouse the view that all understandings are equally valid, for example when they are interpreting evocative texts. This attitude reflects common views in the sociopolitical realm. Seyal Ban-Habib coins this overall stance *situated universality*.[13] Students with such

---

alternative to the ways Western culture conceptualizes moral education and its connection to the growth of autonomous individuals. See Claire Elise Katz, *Levinas and the Crisis of Humanism* (Bloomington: Indiana University Press, 2013). Further research might explore the extent to which the characteristics of attuned learning resonate with these orientations.

[13]   Seyla Ben-Habib, *Situating the Self: Gender, Community and Postmodernism in Contemporary Ethics* (New York: Routledge, 1992), 3. An additional aspect of this attitude lies in the use of the word "respect," when it is interpreted to refer only to the other's right to express herself. In dialogic theories, however, respect for another does not allow for non-engagement but requires careful observation: "To respect someone is to look for the springs that feed the pool of their experience" (William Isaacs, *Dialogue and the Art of Thinking Together* [New York: Doubleday, 1999], 110).

relativist approaches hold that there are no common, objective criteria by which interpretations can be evaluated; consequently, all opinions are seen as equally valid, forestalling the possibility of any further rational discussion, or comparative or qualitative evaluation.[14] Students who adopt such an approach sometimes become very defensive of their own interpretations, leading them to a more reductionist approach. While this may at first glance appear to be in conflict with the idea that all interpretations are equal, it reflects the reality that, among equals, a given learner will be overly committed to her own interpretation—to the point of being closed to other possibilities—because she sees it as an expression of her very self. Thus the subtext that undermines argumentative learning renders as follows: Since interpretation reflects the reader's reading of herself into the text, to question the validity or the quality of an interpretation is perceived as questioning the learner's right to express her personal view. Alternatively, it implies the questioning of her persona, her beliefs, and her value as a human being. These students thus tend to perceive any criticism or questioning as a lack of respect or, worse, a personal attack.

Other students, who cheerily engage in argumentation, often model their approach after the great number of argumentative exchanges in the public (e.g., talk shows) and political realms that take the form of "debates" or "discussions." While being a hallmark of these exchanges, the confrontation of ideas plays a very different role than the way it ideally should in learning conversations. In public/political exchanges, the person who is being challenged experiences a conflicting view as something that she has to overcome, lest she leave the debate seeming weakened or even defeated. For instance, it is very unlikely that students have ever heard a politician say, in the midst of a public debate, "You've

---

14   Jean-François Lyotard, *The Postmodern Condition: A Report on Knowledge*, in *Theory and History of Literature* 10, ed. Wlad Godzich and Jochen Schulte-Sasse (Manchester: Manchester University Press, 1984). The deeper cultural background of such attitudes is rooted in postmodern culture, and in the loss of "grand narratives." See also Jean-François Lyotard, *The Postmodern Explained to Children: Correspondence, 1982–1985* (London: Turnaround, 1992).

presented a very compelling argument. You've convinced me. I now look at the matter differently and may have to revise my position."

The ideas unearthed in the rabbinic texts call attention to the cultural-educational challenge of wanting to cultivate forceful argumentative exchanges that are geared toward mastering the topic at hand. They suggest the need for a clarification of the differences between the acknowledgment of people's different perspectives and the *educational* value of argumentation in the pursuit of understanding.[15] More broadly, they call for a critical and refined examination of the differences between the norms and aims of discussions in educational settings in contrast to those modeled in the public and political realms.[16]

Another idea that emanates from these rabbinic texts is the need to learn to cope with the emotional effects of argumentative learning. Arrogance, as well as the desire to win the argument at all costs, may be fueled by the learner's success in argumentation. Attuned learning therefore calls for the cultivation of "humble righteousness" and mutual goodwill in analyzing and seeking to understand the subject matter. To do so, attuned learners must be able to identify and modulate their own attitudes rather than being subject to them.

Finally, the legend of Resh Lakish and Rabbi Yochanan emphasizes that co-learning should fulfill more than self-serving purposes; it should also consist of a responsibility and a genuine caring for the partner's learning. Both of these aspects of attuned learning are only possible on the basis of a refined awareness of one's own emotions and the other's needs. In addition to the challenges of an individualistic culture as discussed in Chapter Three, here it is noteworthy that while research on digital technology's impact

---

[15] For an example of a pedagogical strategy to help students constructively learn from argumentation in the interpretation of texts, see Holzer with Kent, *A Philosophy of Havruta*, 144–166.

[16] On the backdrop of these ideas, Lyotard's analysis of the increasingly "performative" character of education in modern society highlights the complexity of aiming to educate students to be attuned argumentative learners, since thinking in the pursuit of "truth" is no longer a central value of education, as it doesn't serve goals of "performativity." See Footnote 33.

on human habits—impacts on the mind, the heart, and the hand—
is mostly at its beginning stages, recent works already show that
the expansion of these "advancements" affects people's ability
to develop what Katherin Hayles calls *deep attention*. Hayles,
a postmodern literary critic, is concerned with the difference
between deep and shallow attention (hyper-reading, deep-reading,
machine-reading), and what it would take to educate the younger
generation to experiences that need libidinal investment, such as
love and friendship.[17] American journalist Nicolas Carr, who has
written extensively on the question of neuroscience and technology,
expands Marshall McLuhan's famous saying about technology—
"The medium is the message"—to underscore the extent to which
technology alters patterns of perception, thinking, comprehension,
and ultimately the ability to be "present."[18] Similarly, social
critics and philosophers, using psychoanalytical theories, provide
insightful analysis regarding the effects of marketing and technology
on young people, such as a growing difficulty in developing deep
self-consciousness, deep thinking, and—particularly relevant—
caring for others in relationships.[19] According to these scholars,

---

[17] Katherine N. Hayles, *How We Think: Digital Media and Contemporary Technogenesis* (Chicago: Chicago University Press, 2012).

[18] Nicholas Carr, *The Shallows: What the Internet Is Doing to Our Brains* (New York: Norton and Company, 2011). In regard to text-based learning, Katherine Hayles, an expert who writes about the history of cybernetics and conducts extensive research in the field of the digital humanities, believes that digital reading is bringing an end to the close reading that was crucial in the traditional study of literature (Katherine Hayles, *How We Think: Digital Media and Contemporary Technogenesis*).

[19] See, for example, Bernard Stiegler, *La Télécratie contre la Démocracie* (Paris: Champs, 2006); Bernard Stiegler, *Reenchanter le Monde* (Paris: Flammarion, 2006); Dany-Robert Dufour, *Le Divin Marché* (Paris: Denoel, 2007); Dany-Robert Dufour, *The Art of Shrinking Heads* (Malden, MA: Polity Press, 2008), 92–119, particularly his discussion of education. Dufour is a philosopher of education who has developed a documented thesis showing how fundamental egoistic tenets of a certain version of liberal economy have slowly taken over the norms of other realms, such as education, making it more and more challenging to educate young people for this kind of ethical responsibility. Dufour likes to point out the radical turn of liberal economy expressed by Adam Smith, in changing what until his time was considered as personal vice

technological tools interrupt mental processes of self-searching and reflection that are indispensable not only to the production and acquisition of knowledge, but also to the development of self-knowledge. While such findings should not be overgeneralized, there is no doubt that digital technology does impact individuals' core experiences of self and of others, and that these developments call for critical reflection to articulate and resituate technology vis-à-vis the psycho-social and cognitive realms—in the context of education—in productive ways.[20]

Teachers' Attuned Teaching

To make. To make a difference. Transformation. As discussed in Chapter Four, the sages' emphasis on the potential transformations of the student, the subject matter, and the teacher projects a view of teaching and learning that cannot and should not be reduced to *technical rationality.* The rabbinic text presented in the chapter

---

into a virtue. Smith's famous lines are: "But man has almost constant occasion for the help of his brethren, and it is in vain for him to expect it from their benevolence only. He will be more likely to prevail if he can interest their self-love in his favor, and show them that it is for their own advantage to do for him what he requires of them. Whoever offers to another a bargain of any kind, proposes to do this. Give me that which I want, and you shall have this which you want, is the meaning of every such offer; and it is in this manner that we obtain from one another the far greater part of those good offices which we stand in need of. It is not from the benevolence of the butcher, the brewer, or the baker that we expect our dinner, but from their regard to their own interest. We address ourselves, not to their humanity but to their self-love, and never talk to them of our own necessities but of their advantages" (Adam Smith, *An Inquiry into the Nature and the Causes of the Wealth of Nations,* ed. Kathryn Sutherland [Oxford: Oxford University Press, 1993] Part I, 22).

[20] These reflections do not express a negative attitude toward the growing use of digital technologies in general and in the context of education in particular. But too often, educational discourse about these technologies is conducted on the premise of the principle "if you can't beat them, join them" and is limited to the ways these technologies can be used in education or to the content that they make accessible. The lack of attention to the deeper psychological and interpersonal impacts (both constructive and harmful) at times seems like the elephant in the room.

primarily addresses the teacher, in raising his awareness of the
importance of students' transformation, suggesting that the
teacher's role is to educate the youngster to become a fuller human
being (notwithstanding the different meanings this could take).
In contrast, there exists a growing skepticism among teachers
and society with regard to the scope and the moral grounds of
the teaching profession. Among the most radical espousers of
this skepticism are a number of social critics whose writings have
had a cultural impact in various societal realms. In the wake of
the cultural protests of the sixties, Michel Foucault associates the
teacher's role with power manipulation, designed to mold young
people in the service of the existing social, ideological, and economic
orders. Thus, schools are among the controlling mechanisms, and
teachers are merely fulfilling the role of its invisible administrative
machinery.[21] Sociologist Pierre Bourdieu undermines teachers'
mandate to educate, asserting that it entails arbitrary cultural
violence: "All pedagogic action is, objectively, symbolic violence
insofar as it is the imposition of a cultural arbitrary by an arbitrary
power."[22]

To be sure, the arguments and analysis leading to these critiques
are enlightening. Originally, the goal of these critiques was to
liberate educational systems from the chains that prevent authentic
individuation.[23] Three to four decades later, new voices point out that

---

21   Michel Foucault, *Discipline and Punish: The Birth of the Prison* (New York:
      Random House, 1975), 186–194.

22   Pierre Bourdieu and Jean-Claude Passeron, *Reproduction in Education, Society
      and Culture* (London: Sage Publications, 2000), 5. Western culture produced
      a number of myths on the fabrication of a human by another human being.
      Pygmalion, the Golem, and Pinocchio are three examples of this ultimate
      dream of education. In contrast, Maria Montessori's famous oxymoron
      conceptualizes education as a child's call: "Help me to help myself."

23   Foucault criticizes the foundations of technical rationality in education: "All
      the sciences, analyses or practices employing the root 'psycho-' have their
      origin in this historical reversal of the procedures of individualization. The
      moment that saw the transition from the historico-ritual mechanisms of the
      formation of the individuality to the scientifico-disciplinary mechanisms,
      when the normal took over from the ancestral, and measurement from status,
      thus substituting for the individuality of the memorable man that of the

undermining the right of schools and teachers to educate brought
about new and less visible forms of alienation of youth, as they have
become less capable of critically and responsibly engaging with the
influences of business-driven role models in social media and with
the impact of primary drives exalted by a consumerist economy.[24]
The time has come to reflect critically on views that identify cultural
transmission and the will to educate with forms of oppression,[25]

calculable man, that moment when the sciences of man became possible is
the moment when a new technology of power and a new political anatomy
of the body were implemented" (Michel Foucault, *Discipline and Punish*, 193).
Schools are perceived as an obstacle to the freedom of the younger person and
to his or her ability to become "him- or herself": "Prisons resemble factories,
schools, barracks, hospitals, which all resemble prisons" (Michel Foucault,
Discipline and Punish, 228).

[24] A couple of insightful analyses of this process by Western European critics
can be found. See, for example, Jean-Claude Michea, *The Teaching of Ignorance
and Its Modern Conditions* (Paris: Climats, 1999). It is fair to assume that
despite the different cultural contexts, similar patterns can be identified in
the American context. For an early critical analysis see Hannah Arendt, "The
Crisis in Education," in *Between Past and Future* (New York: Penguin, 1968),
173–196.

[25] Such reflection will have to go back and discuss Immanuel Kant's view,
according to which the human being is the only animal that has to be
educated with the assistance of the previous generation: "All the natural
endowments of mankind must be developed little by little out of man
himself, through his own effort. One generation educates the next"
(Buchner, *Educational Theory of Immanuel Kant*, 2–3). See also "It is only
through the efforts of people of broader views, who take an interest
in the universal good, and who are capable of entertaining the idea of
a better condition of things in the future, that the gradual progress of
human nature towards its goal is possible" (ibid., 17). On the basis of other
philosophical traditions, especially in the realm of Jewish religious education,
such reflection also will engage with Emmanuel Levinas, whose philosophy
offers a radically alternative way to think about education, human autonomy,
and ethics (Katz, *Levinas and the Crisis of Humanism*) and the writings of
Abraham Joshua Heschel. See, for example: "The failure of Jewish education
has its roots in the failure of *faith in Jewish education*, and ultimately in the
failure of faith in value education. Our premise is the certainty of being able to
educate the inner man, to form as well as to inform the personality, to develop
not only memory but also the capacity for insight, not only information but
also appreciation, not only proficiency but also reverence, not only learning,
but also faith, not only skills but also a *sense of values*" (Heschel, "The Values
of Jewish Education," 27).

especially as we approach what seems an almost inevitable and radical change in the educational formulation of classrooms and school buildings in the wake of new options offered by the digital revolution and relevant economic considerations.[26]

In a similar vein, some educators who consider themselves progressive and/or dialogical teachers are uncomfortable with Resh Lakish's assertion that a teacher "makes" a student. Deliberately aiming to transform the student into someone different undermines all they believed in as teachers who first and foremost want to be respectful of students' autonomy. On the other hand, John Dewey felt uncomfortable with teachers' refusal to engage proactively in teaching so as not to infringe on student's development of independent thinking. He writes:

> There is a present tendency in so-called advanced schools of educational thought to say, in effect, let us surround pupils with certain materials, tools, appliances, etc., and then let the pupils respond to these things according to their own desires. Above all let us not suggest any end or plan to the students; let us not suggest to them what they shall do, for that is an unwarranted trespass upon their sacred intellectual individuality since the essence of such individuality is to set up ends and aims. Now such a method is really stupid. For it attempts the impossible, which is always stupid; and it misconceives the conditions of independent thinking.[27]

Martin Buber strongly criticizes educators' understanding of child-centered pedagogy as a renunciation of character formation.[28] Paulo Freire, in support of educators re-engagement with teaching as transformation, demonstrates a common misinterpretation of his dialogical pedagogy. First, he points out, there is a need to

---

[26]   Such directions are critically explored in the works of French philosopher Marcel Gauchet. Particularly in his recent book: Marie Claude Blais, Marcel Gauchet, and Dominique Ottavi, *Transmettre, Apprendre* (Paris: Stock, 2014).

[27]   Joseph Ratner, ed., *Intelligence in the Modern World: John Dewey's Philosophy* (New York: The Modern Library, 1939), 623–624.

[28]   "Education worthy of the name is essentially education in character" (Buber, *Between Man and Man*, 104).

distinguish between *facilitation* and *teaching.* Failing to do so is a form of moral self-deceit:

> When teachers call themselves facilitators and not teachers, they become involved in a distortion of reality. To begin with, in de-emphasizing the teacher's power by claiming to be a facilitator, one is being less than truthful to the extent that the teacher turned facilitator maintains the power institutionally created in the position. That is, while facilitators may veil their power, at any moment they can exercise power as they wish. The facilitator still grades, still has certain control over the curriculum, and to deny these facts is to be disingenuous.[29]

Teachers should learn to differentiate between authoritarianism and authority. The former—a teacher's self-serving use of authority—is indeed to be rejected; but the latter is essential to education: "The teacher who claims to be a facilitator and not a teacher is renouncing, for reasons unbeknownst to us, the task of teaching and, hence, the task of dialogue." Similarly, Freire criticizes teachers' tendency to empty their role of any directive elements. For Freire, this is deceitful:

> I do not think that there is real education without direction. To the extent that all educational practice brings with itself its own transcendence, it presupposes an objective to be reached. Therefore, practice cannot be nondirective. There is no educational practice that does not point to an objective; this proves that the nature of educational practice has direction. The facilitator who claims that "since I respect students I cannot be directive, and since they are individuals deserving respect, they should determine their own direction," does not deny the directive nature of education that is independent of his own subjectivity. Rather, this facilitator denies himself or herself the pedagogical, political, and epistemological task of assuming the role of a subject of that directive practice. This facilitator refuses to convince his or her learners of what he or she thinks is just. This educator, then, ends up helping the power structure. To avoid reproducing the

---

[29] Paulo Freire and Donaldo P. Macedo, "A Dialogue: Culture, Language, and Race," *Harvard Educational Review* 65, no. 3 (1995), 378.

values of the power structure, the educator must always combat a laissez-faire pedagogy, no matter how progressive it may appear to be.[30]

Finally, in his dialogical approach to teaching, Freire evokes something of teachers' attunement to students' transformation. Teaching for transformation requires a heightened presence together with self-critical awareness, so that the teacher's effort to transform the learner will not be at the price of the student's inner growth:

> The radical educator has to be an active presence in educational practice. But, educators should never allow their active and curious presence to transform the learners' presence into a shadow of the educator's presence. Nor can educators be a shadow of their learners. The educator who dares to teach has to stimulate learners to live a critically conscious presence in the pedagogical and historical process.[31]

Afterword

With the formal establishment of mass and public education throughout the last century and a half, specialized and scientific-based knowledge have slowly but surely come to determine educational discourse. Education has increasingly become *reflexive* in the sense that Anthony Giddens defines that term: it develops and is impacted by scientific bodies of knowledge such as the realms of child psychology, pedagogical methods, or the understanding

---

[30]   Ibid.

[31]   Ibid., 379. A little further into that article, Freire's colleague Macedo adds another requirement for a dialogue to be educational, which seems most relevant today: "The object of knowledge is the fundamental goal, the dialogue as conversation about individuals' lived experiences does not truly constitute dialogue. In other words, the appropriation of the notion of dialogical teaching as a process of sharing experiences creates a situation in which teaching is reduced to a form of group therapy that focuses on the psychology of the individual [. . .] Simply put, I do not think that the sharing of experiences should be understood in psychological terms only" (380).

of social mechanisms.[32] In regard to the practice of teaching, three decades ago Donald Schon denounced the "crisis of confidence in professional knowledge" as educational discourse was surrendering to *technical rationality*, an epistemology of professional practice according to which "professional activity consists in instrumental problem solving made rigorous by the application of scientific theory and technique."[33] Subsumed by the logic of competencies, education is less and less conceptualized by its specific expectations such as the development of rational and critical human beings who are morally responsible and capable of intimate relationships.

In 1979, in a book that originated in a report on education and knowledge commissioned by Québec's Ministry of Higher Education, philosopher and analyst of postmodern Western culture Jean-François Lyotard describes a substantial mutation in the idea of education. In a section called "Education and Its Legitimation through Performativity," he explains that the concept of *utility* has replaced the idea of *truth* as the supreme value of educational thinking. Education is evaluated in regard to its optimal contribution to "the best performativity of the social system. Accordingly it will educate people with the skills that are indispensable to that system."[34] Lyotard concludes that the general effect of performativity is the subordination of higher learning institutions to the existing economic powers so that "the moment knowledge ceases to be an end in itself—the realization of the Idea or the emancipation of

---

[32] Anthony Giddens, *The Consequences of Modernity* (Cambridge: Polity Press, 1990).

[33] Donald A. Schon, *The Reflective Practitioner: How Professionals Think in Action* (USA: Basic Books, 1983), 21. At the same time, while the turn to this ideology of professionalism—writes Lee Shulman—valued the technical, objective, and scientific, it also had an equally strong moral and service aspect that we need to recover: Lee S. Shulman, "Theory, Practice and the Education of Professionals," *The Elementary School Journal* 98, no. 5 (1998): 511–526.

[34] Jean-François Lyotard, "The Postmodern Condition: A Report on Knowledge," 48. Compare to Jean Jacques Rousseau's famous lines reflecting humanist education: "How to live is the business I wish to teach him. On leaving my hands he will not, I admit, be a magistrate, a soldier, or a priest; first of all he will be a man" (Jean Jacques Rousseau, *Emile or Concerning Education* [Boston: Heath and Company, 1889], 13–14).

men—its transmission is no longer the exclusive responsibility of scholars and students."[35]

Martha Nussbaum warns about the breakdown of the humanities in today's education. She writes:

> We are in the midst of a crisis of massive proportions and grave global significance. . . . I mean a crisis that goes largely unnoticed, like a cancer; a crisis that is likely to be, in the long run, far more damaging to the future of democratic self-government: a worldwide crisis in education. Radical changes are occurring in what democratic societies teach the young, and these changes have not been well thought through. Thirsty for national profit, nations, and their systems of education, are heedlessly discarding skills that are needed to keep democracies alive. If this trend continues, nations all over the world will soon be producing generations of useful machines, rather than complete citizens who can think for themselves, criticize tradition, and understand the significance of another person's sufferings and achievements. The future of the world's democracies hangs in the balance.[36]

According to Nussbaum, economic growth has brought societies to invest in thinking about education at the expense of actually educating them in ways that are fundamental to secure them as democratic citizens. Nussbaum points to abilities that she associates with the humanities and the arts: "the ability to think critically; the ability to transcend local loyalties and to approach world problems as 'citizen of the world'; and finally, to imagine sympathetically the predicament of another person."[37]

Scholars argue with Nussbaum's beliefs about the educational power of the humanities and about the purposes that humanities can or cannot serve.[38] But in my view, it is not only the ousting

---

[35]   Ibid., 50.

[36]   Martha C. Nussbaum, *Not for Profit: Why Democracy Needs the Humanities* (Princeton: Princeton University Press, 2010), 6–7.

[37]   Ibid., 7.

[38]   For the controversy on the role of humanities to achieve such goals, see, for example, Stanley Fish, "A Classical Education: Back to the Future," *The New York Times*, June 7, 2010, http://opinionator.blogs.nytimes.com/2010/06/07/a-classical-education-back-to-the-future.

of the humanities but perhaps, in a more subtle way, something of the all-embracing impact of the economic and technical ethos that is impacting and redefining value systems, political, semiotic, and symbolic realms as well as educational discourse. Perhaps more than anything else—it changes the profile of the child whom teachers meet in the classroom, as implied by Lyotard and others.[39]

In the face of these complex societal and cultural processes, the views of teaching, learning, student, teacher, and co-learner that are encapsulated in attuned learning may appear as disruptive in their content, and rather simplistic in their expression. Furthermore, it may well be that the language of habits of the heart and mindfulness may appear to be better suited to an advertisement for a weekend retreat than to everyday learning settings. But perhaps it is by refining our awareness, and reconnecting with subtler dimensions of the wonder of teaching and learning, that it will be possible to carve out new paths for education to be a fundamentally human and humanizing activity in the present:

> What do I do when I teach? I talk.
>
> I have no other way of making a living and I have no other dignity; I have no other way of transforming the world and no other influence on other people.

---

[39]   The impact of economic and technological realms on all other realms of human life is discussed by a number of scholars including philosopher Gilbert Simondon, "The Genesis of the Individual," in *Incorporations*, ed. Jonathan Crary and Sanford Kwinter (New York: Zone Books, 1992), 297–319; Gilbert Simondon, *L'individu et sa genèse physico-biologique* (Paris: PUF, 1964). See also: "In truth, we are touching here upon a fundamental factor, one that the great political thinkers of the past knew and that the alleged 'political philosophers' of today, bad sociologists and poor theoreticians, splendidly ignore: the intimate solidarity between a social regime and the anthropological type (or the spectrum of such types) needed to make it function. For the most part, capitalism has inherited these anthropological types from previous historical periods: the incorruptible judge, the Weberian civil servant, the teacher devoted to his task, the worker whose work was, in spite of everything, a source of pride. Such personalities are becoming inconceivable in the contemporary age: it is not clear why today they would be reproduced, who would reproduce them, and in the name of what they would function" (Cornelius Castoriadis, *The Rising Tide of Insignificancy*, http://www.notbored. org/RTI.pdf, 137–138).

Speaking is my work: language is my kingdom.

My students, for the most part, will have another relation with things and with people; they will construct something with their hands; or perhaps they will speak and write in businesses, in stores, in administrative offices, but their language will not be the language which teaches. It will be part of an action, an order, a plan, or the beginning of an action.

My speaking does not begin any action, it does not command any action which can be involved, directly or indirectly, in any production. I speak only to communicate to the younger generation the knowledge and the research of the older generation.

This communication by speech of acquired knowledge and research in progress is my reason for being, my profession, and my honor. I am not jealous of those who are "in the real world" who have "a grip on reality," as are certain teachers who are unhappy with themselves. My reality and my life is the kingdom of words, of sentences, and of discourse itself.[40]

***

It is wrong to define education as preparation for life. Learning *is* life, a supreme experience of living, a climax of existence. The teacher is more than a technician. He is the representative as well as the interpreter of mankind's most sacred possessions. Learning is holy, an indispensable form of purification as well as ennoblement. By learning I do not mean memorization, erudition,—I mean the very act of study, of being involved in wisdom.[41]

---

[40] Paul Ricoeur, "Language is my Kingdom," trans. Charles E. Reagan, *Esprit* 23 (1955): 192.

[41] Abraham Joshua Heschel, "Children and Youth," in *The Insecurity of Freedom: Essays on Human Existence* (New York: Farrar, Strauss and Giroux, 1967), 42.

Academies

Talmudic academies, which existed in both Israel and Babylon, served as centers for Jewish scholarship and the development of Jewish law. The academies had a lasting impact on the development of rabbinic Judaism, including the creation of the Jerusalem Talmud and the Babylonian Talmud. The schools (or "houses") of Hillel and Shammai are two academies reported to have been thriving in the first century, before the destruction of the Second Temple. The Talmud reports hundreds of their disagreements and debates on legal questions, biblical exegesis, and religious philosophy.

Aggadah (plural, aggadot)

Aggadah translates literally as "tales." It refers to the homiletic and non-legalistic exegetical texts in the classical rabbinic literature of Judaism, particularly as recorded in the Talmud and Midrash. In general, aggadah is a compendium of rabbinic homilies that incorporates folklore, legends about scholars, historical anecdotes, moral exhortations, and practical advice in various spheres of life. See also *midrash aggadah;* contrast to *halacha.*

Beit (ha)midrash

Literally the "house of study" or "house of interpretation." The beit (ha)midrash refers to the study hall located in a Talmudic academy, a synagogue, or another location. People study in pairs or in small groups. The origin of the beit midrash can be traced to the early rabbinic period, following the siege of Jerusalem (70 C.E.). Early rabbinic literature, including the Mishnah, makes mention of the beit midrash as an institution meant as a place of Torah study and interpretation, as well as the development of halacha.

Chavruta (havruta, hevruta)

Chavruta means "companionship" or "friendship." It is an extension of the Hebrew word chaver, "companion" or "friend," and is used in reference to paired or small group study. In its common use, the word chavruta can refer to the learning pair, to the learning partner, and/or to the practice of paired learning itself.

Dispositions

In this book, "disposition" indicates a habit, a state of readiness, or a tendency to act in a specified way. The virtues and vices that comprise one's moral character are typically understood as dispositions to behave in certain ways in various circumstances. Dispositions are understood to be relatively stable, long-term, and consistent across a wide spectrum of conditions. Ethical dispositions indicate the marriage between skills and attitudes in regard to moral virtues. For instance, an honest person is disposed to telling the truth when asked.

Halacha (adjective, halachic)

Unless indicated otherwise, throughout the word halacha means "Jewish law" in the context of this book. Halacha (derived from a root meaning "to go" or "to walk") is Judaism's collective body of religious law, comprised of the biblical commandments and subsequent Talmudic and rabbinic laws and customs. The term halacha also refers to the practical application of Jewish law. Halachic process refers to the discussions, disagreements, and (re) interpretation, and ruling processes of the laws' implementation in new and changing contexts. Halacha is studied, developed, and applied by various halachic authorities, often scholars who hold no formal communal, juridical, or political position in the community but who are recognized for their wisdom. It should be noted that Jewish legal tradition does not distinguish between what many would consider religious and non-religious life, such that halacha guides not only religious practices and beliefs, but all aspects of day-to-day functioning. Halacha is contrasted with aggadah, the diverse corpus of rabbinic exegetical, narrative, philosophical, mystical, and other non-legal texts, and there exist dynamic interchanges between the two genres. Halacha is the subject of ongoing study by both scholars and laypeople, not necessarily for practical or ruling purposes. This is exemplified in the study of Talmud, which serves as a major source of halachic literature.

Hanassi, Rabbi Yehuda

Literally, "Yehuda [Judah] the Prince," also known in rabbinic literature as "Rabbi," is a second-century sage (c. 135–217 CE) and leader of the Jewish community in Israel during the Roman occupation of Judea. Yehuda the Prince is recognized in rabbinic tradition as the formal redactor and editor of the Mishna.

Hasidism

Hasidism is a branch of Orthodox Judaism that promotes spirituality through the popularization and internalization of Jewish mysticism as the fundamental aspect of the faith. (The Hebrew, *Hasidut*, stands for "piety" or "lovingkindness.") It was founded in eighteenth-century Eastern Europe by Rabbi Yisrael Baal Shem Tov (circa 1700–1760), who sought to awaken a popular, mystical revival for the simple Jewish folk, as well as offering scholarly mysticism a new soulful direction. The teachings of Hasidism look to the simple, inner divine soul, which it sees as permeating all and also transcending all. Hasidic thought is based on earlier mystical theology, but its ideas relate to human psychology and experience, so that Jewish mysticism can awaken a personal experience and perception of the divine. In most Hasidic dynasties, Hasidism stressed a doctrine of the *rebbe* or *tzaddik* (saintly leader), through whom divine influence is channeled. In some Hasidic paths the tzaddik elevates his followers through charismatic conduct, while other groups emphasize his role primarily as teacher.

Midrash, midrash aggadah

Midrash is the body of exegesis of Torah texts along with homiletical stories that provide an intrinsic analysis of biblical passages. *Midrash* comes from the root *darash (dalet resh shin)*—"to seek," to study," "to inquire." Midrash is a method of interpreting biblical stories that goes beyond a simple distillation of religious, legal, or moral teachings. Midrash may resolve problems in the interpretation of difficult passages of the Bible, using principles of interpretation, and may teach religious and ethical values. Broadly defined, midrash is divided in two major categories: halachic (legal) or aggadic (non-legal and chiefly homiletic). They are assembled in different compilations, dating from the second century through the Middle Ages. This book refers to midrashic teachings included in the Talmud (e.g., in Chapter Three) as well as in separate post-Talmudic compilations (e.g., Chapter Six).

Rabbinics, rabbinic literature

In contemporary academic writing, both terms often refer specifically to rabbinic writings from the Talmudic era, as opposed to medieval or modern rabbinic writing. In their broadest sense, however, these terms can mean the entire spectrum of rabbinic writings throughout Jewish history. This book intends the broad sense and provides the historical dates of the characters.

Sage (talmid chacham)

Talmid chacham ("wise student") is an honorific title given to one well versed in Jewish law, the knowledgeable interpreter and generator of new knowledge—in effect, a Torah scholar. This book refers to the protagonists of rabbinic literature as "sages" rather than the conventional title of "rabbis," unless explicitly mentioned in the rabbinic text. Today the title "rabbi" generally connotes a public official and a community leader.

The Sages (Chazal)

"The Sages" is a general term that refers to all Jewish sages of the Mishna and Talmud or, more broadly, all those between the first and the sixth centuries CE. In Hebrew, they are referred as *Chazal*, an acronym for the Hebrew "Chachameinu Zichronam Livracha" ("Our Sages, of blessed memory").

Shechina

Shechina is a noun meaning "dwelling" or "settling," which denotes the dwelling or settling of the Divine Presence. Proximity to the Shehina makes the connection to God more readily perceivable.

Sugyot (singular, *sugya*)

A *sugya* is a chapter section in the Talmud, which typically comprises a detailed proof-based elaboration of a legal statement.

Talmud

The Talmud (a word meaning "instruction" and "learning") refers to two works, the Jerusalem Talmud (edited in the fourth century BCE, and also known as the "Palestinian Talmud," as the area had been renamed "Palestine" by the Roman conquerors) and the Babylonian Talmud (edited throughout and beyond the fifth century BCE). When used alone, the word *Talmud* generally denotes the Babylonian Talmud. The Talmud serves as the basis for all codes of Jewish law and is the focus of ongoing study by traditional Jews. It has two components: the Mishna (circa 220 BCE), which is a compilation of legal opinions, and the Gemara, which includes interpretation and elaboration of the Mishna and additional rabbinic writings, including on esoteric aspects of life, Jewish ethics, civil and religious law, legal analysis, rituals, philosophy, customs, etc. Traditionally, Talmudic statements are classified into two broad categories, halachic and aggadic. Halachic statements directly relate to questions of Jewish law and practice while aggadic statements are not related to legalities, but rather are exegetical, homiletical, ethical, or historical in nature. Both the Babylonian and Jerusalem Talmud are divided into tractates, chapters, and page numbers (the letters "a" and "b" referring to the front and back pages of a leaf). The various printed editions have preserved the traditional page division so that all references annotate the tractate and the page number.

Talmud Torah

Literally, the study of Torah. The term carries two meanings: 1) a form of private primary school that gave boys an elementary education in Hebrew, the Pentateuch, and the Talmud. 2) In rabbinic literature, the religious obligation to study Torah, and in a broader sense, the field of study that deals with Jewish law.

Torah

Torah means "instruction," and it offers a way of life for those who follow it. The term is used in a range of meanings to indicate the Pentateuch and the twenty-four books of the Jewish Bible. In rabbinic literature, it also denotes the Oral Torah, which consists of interpretations and amplifications that, according to rabbinic tradition, have been handed down from generation to generation and are now embodied in the Talmud and in the midrash.

Torah lishmah

Torah lishmah is a rabbinic concept that translates as "Torah study for its own sake." *Lishmah* refers to a sense of purity of a person's motivation and intention when he engages in Torah study. Lishmah is taken by some to refer to the functional purpose of Torah study — to enable the performance and observance of religious life. A second strain of the term lishmah refers to the pious motive to serve and glorify God. Torah study, when performed unselfishly, out of true love of God, is then depicted as the highest form of religious consciousness. Rabbi Chaim of Volozhin (1749–1821) developed a theory that lishmah connotes the study of Torah for the very sake of Torah study, that is to acquire more knowledge of God's will. The purest motive for Torah study must be internal — to become more adept in its logic and more knowledgeable of its vastness. Thus the study of Torah demands undisturbed focus and exhaustive mental energy. To varying degrees, modern Torah study has witnessed a process of diversification, but one that still assigns Torah study not just the highest ethical value, but also views it as the practice that can, optimally, facilitate comprehensive religious and moral development.

Bibliography

Aberbach, Moses. "The Relations Between Master and Disciple in the Talmudic Age." In *Essays Presented to Chief Rabbi Israel Brodie*, edited by Hirsch Jakob Zimmels, Joseph Rabbinowitz, and Israel Finestein, 1–24. London: Soncino Press, 1967.

Abrabanel, Isaac. *Nachalat Avot*. New York: Silberman, 1953. (Hebrew)

Almaas, A-Hameed. *Essence: The Diamond Approach to Inner Realization*. York Beach: Samuel Weiser, 1986.

— —. *The Unfolding Now: Realizing Your True Nature through the Practice of Presence*. Boston and London: Shambala, 2008.

Althusser, Louis and Étienne Balibar. *Reading Capital*. London: NLB, 1970.

Apel, Karl-Otto. "The Problem of Philosophical Foundations in Light of Transcendental Pragmatics of Language." In *After Philosophy: End or Transformation?*, edited by Kenneth Baynes and James Bohman, 250–299. Cambridge, MA: MIT Press, 1987.

Arendt, Hannah. "The Crisis in Education." In *Between Past and Future*, 173–196. New York: Penguin, 1968.

Arthur, James, Ian Davies, and Carole Hahn, eds. *SAGE Handbook of Education for Citizenship and Democracy*. Thousand Oaks: Sage Publications, 2008.

Assaf, Simha. *Mekorot Letoldot Hahinukh beYisra'el: Mitehilat Yemehabenayim ad Tekufat Hahaskalah (A Source-Book for the History of Jewish Education from the Beginning of the Middle Ages to the Period of the Haskalah)*. Tel Aviv: Devir, 1925. (Hebrew)

Assaf, Simha and Shmuel Glick, eds. *Mekorot Letoldot Hachinuch Hayehudi*. New York: Beit Hamidrash Lerabbanim, 2001. (Hebrew)

Azulay, Haim Yossef David. *Petach Eynayim*, vol. 1. Jerusalem: Makor, 1959. (Hebrew)

Ball, Deborah L. and David K. Cohen. "Developing Practice, Developing Practitioners, Toward a Practice-Based Theory of Professional Education." In *Teaching as the Learning Profession: Handbook of Policy and Practice*, edited by Linda Darling-Hammond and Gary Sykes, 3–32. San Francisco: Jossey-Bass, 1999.

Banon, David. *La Lecture Infinie: Les Voies de l'Interpretation Midrashique*. Paris: Du Seuil, 1987. (French)

Baudelaire, Charles. *Paris Spleen: Little Poems in Prose*. Middletown: Wesleyan University Press, 2010.

Bauman, Zygmunt. *Life in Fragments: Essays in Postmodern Morality*. Oxford: Blackwell Publishers, 1995.

Baumeister, Roy. "How the Self Became a Problem: A Psychological Review of Historical Research." *Journal of Personality and Social Psychology* 52, no. 1 (1987): 163–176.

Bellah, Robert N. et al. *The Good Society*. New York: Vintage Books, 1991.

— —. *Habits of the Heart: Individualism and Commitment in American Life*. Berkeley: University of California Press, 2007.

Ben-Habib, Seyla. *Situating the Self: Gender, Community and Postmodernism in Contemporary Ethics*. New York: Routledge, 1992.

Bingham, Charles and Alexander M. Sidorkin. *No Education without Relation*. New York: Peter Lang, 2004.

Blais, Marie-Claude, Marcel Gauchet, and Dominique Ottavi. *Transmettre, Apprendre*. Paris: Stock, 2014. (French)

Bourdieu, Pierre and Jean-Claude Passeron. *Reproduction in Education, Society and Culture*. London: Sage Publications, 2000.

Boyarin, Daniel. *Carnal Israel: Reading Sex in Talmudic Culture*. Berkeley and Los Angeles: University of California Press, 1995.

— —. *Intertextuality and the Reading of Midrash*. Bloomington: Indiana University Press, 1990.

Boyd, Ray, Neil MacNeill, and Greg Sullivan. "Relational Pedagogy: Putting Balance Back Into Students' Learning." *Curriculum Leadership* 4, no. 13 (2006): 1–5.

Breuer, Mordechai. *Ohale Torah: Hayeshiva Tavnita Vetoldoteha*. Jerusalem: Merkaz Zalman Shazar Publication, 2003. (Hebrew)

Brewer, Charles L. "Reflections on an Academic Career: From Which Side of the Looking Glass?" In *The Teaching of Psychology: Essays in Honor of Wilbert J. McKeachie and Charles L. Brewer*, edited by Stephen F. Davis and William Buskist, 499–507. Mahwah, NJ: Lawrence Erlbaum Associates, 2002.

Brophy, Jere and Thomas Good. *Teacher-Student Relationships*. New York: Holt, Rinehart and Winston, 1974.

Brown, Kirk Warren and Richard M. Ryan. "The Benefits of Being Present: Mindfulness and its Role in Psychological Well-being." *Journal of Personality and Social Psychology* 84, no. 4 (2003): 822–848.

Brown, Peter. *The World of Late Antiquity: From Marcus Aurelius to Muhammad (AD 150–750)*. United Kingdom: Thames and Hudson, 1989.

Buber, Martin. *Between Man and Man*. New York: McMillan, 1965.

— —. "Elements of the Interhuman." In *Martin Buber: The Knowledge of Man; Selected Essays*, edited by Maurice Friedman, 68–87. Baltimore: Humanity Books, 1988.

— —. *I and Thou*. New York: Charles Scribner's Sons, 1970.

Buchner, Edward F., ed. and trans. *Educational Theory of Immanuel Kant.* New York: AMS Press, 1971.

Burbules, Nicholas C. "Navigating the Advantages and Disadvantages of Online Pedagogy." In *Learning, Culture and Community in Online Education: Research and Practice*, edited by Caroline Haythornthwaite and Michelle M. Kazmer, 3–17. New York: Peter Lang Publishing, 2004.

Burbules, Nicholas C. and C. Bruce Bertram. "Theory and Research on Teaching as Dialogue." In *Handbook of Research on Teaching*, 4th ed., edited by Virginia Richardson, 1102–1121. Washington, DC: American Educational Research Association, 2001.

Calderon, Ruth. *Hashuck.Habayit. Halev: Aggadot Talmudiot.* Jerusalem: Keter Publishing, 2001. (Hebrew)

Camus, Albert. *The First Man.* New York: Alfred A. Knopf, 1995.

Carr, David. "Rival Conceptions of Practice in Education and Teaching." *Journal of Philosophy of Education* 37, no. 2 (2003): 253–266.

Carr, Nicholas. *The Shallows: What the Internet is Doing to Our Brains.* New York: Norton and Company, 2011.

Castoriadis, Cornelius. *The Rising Tide of Insignifancy.* http://www.notbored.org/RTI.pdf.

Christensen, C. Roland, David A. Garvin, and Ann Sweet, eds. *Education for Judgment: The Artistry of Discussion Leadership.* Cambridge, Massachusetts: Harvard Business School, 1991.

Cohen, Jonathan and Elie Holzer, eds. *Modes of Educational Translation: Studies in Jewish Education.* Jerusalem: Magnes Press, 2009.

Cohen, Richard A. "The Face of Truth in Rosenzweig, Levinas, and Jewish Mysticism." In *Phenomenology of the Truth Proper to Religion*, edited by Daniel Guerrière, 175–201. New York: SUNY Press, 1990.

Collingwood, Robin G. *The Principles of Art.* Oxford: Oxford University Press, 1958.

Connely, F. Michael and D. Jean Clandinin. *Teachers as Curriculum Planners: Narratives of Experience.* New York: Teachers College Press, 1988.

Cranton, Patricia and Edward W. Taylor, eds. *The Handbook of Transformative Learning: Theory, Research, and Practice.* Hoboken: John Wiley & Sons, 2012.

Damasio, Antonio. *The Feeling of What Happens: Body and Emotion in the Making of Consciousness.* London: Heinemann, 1999.

Davey, Nicholas. *Unquiet Understanding: Gadamer's Philosophical Hermeneutics.* Albany: State University of New York Press, 2006.

Deiro, Judith A. *Teaching with Heart: Making Healthy Connections with Students.* Thousand Oaks: Corwin Press, 1996.

DePaul, Michael R. "Argument and Perception: The Role of Literature in Moral Inquiry." *Journal of Philosophy* 85, no. 10 (1988): 552–565.

Derber, Charles. *The Pursuit of Attention: Power and Individualism in Everyday Life*. Oxford: Oxford University Press, 1979.

Dewey, John. *Democracy and Education*. New York: McMillan, 1916.

——. *Experience and Education*. Toronto: Collier-Books, 1963.

——. *Human Nature and Conduct*. New York: Modern Library, 1957.

Dirkx, John M. "Nurturing Soul Work: A Jungian Approach to Transformative Learning." In *The Handbook of Transformative Learning: Theory, Research, and Practice*, edited by Patricia C. Cranton and Edward W. Taylor, 116–129. Hoboken: John Wiley & Sons, 2012.

——. "Transformative Learning Theory in the Practice of Adult Education: An Overview." *PAACE Journal of Lifelong Learning* 7 (1998): 1–14.

Donahue, David M. "Conflict as a Constructive Curricular Strategy." In *Democratic Dilemmas of Teaching Service-Learning: Curricular Strategies for Success*, edited by Christine M. Cress, David M. Donahue, and Associates, 101–109. Virginia: Stylus Publishing LLC, 2011.

Donoghue, Denis. *The Practice of Reading*. New Haven: Yale University Press, 1998. Dorph, Gail Z. and Barry W. Holtz. "Professional Development for Teachers: Why Doesn't the Model Change?" *Journal of Jewish Education* 66, no. 2 (2000): 67–76.

Dreyfus, Georges B. J. *The Sound of Two Hands Clapping: The Education of a Tibetan Buddhist Monk*. Berkeley: University California Press, 2003.

Dufour, Dany-Robert. *The Art of Shrinking Heads*. Malden: Polity Press, 2008.

——. *Le Divin Marché*. Paris: Denoel, 2007. (French)

Dunne, Joseph. *Back to the Rough Ground: Practical Judgment and the Lure of Technique*. Notre Dame: University of Notre Dame Press, 2001.

Durkheim, Emile. *Education and Sociology*. New York: The Free Press, 1956.

——. *Suicide*. New York: Free Press, 1951.

Eagleton, Terry. *After Theory*. New York: Basic Books, 2003.

Eco, Umberto. *The Role of the Reader: Exploration in the Semiotics of Texts*. Bloomington: Indiana University Press, 1979.

Ekman, Paul. "Facial Expressions." In *Handbook of Cognition and Emotion*, edited by Tim Dalgleish and Mick Power, 301–320. West Sussex, England: John Wiley and Sons Ltd., 1999.

Elias, David. "It's Time to Change Our Minds: An Introduction to Transformative Learning." *ReVision* 20, no. 1 (1997): 2–6.

Elman, Yaakov and Israel Gershoni. *Transmitting Jewish Traditions: Orality, Textuality and Cultural Diffusion*. New Haven and London: Yale University Press, 2000.

Faulkner, Dorothy. *Learning Relationships in the Classroom*. London: Routledge, 1998.

Feiman-Nemser, Sharon. "Beit Midrash for Teachers: An Experiment in Teacher Preparation." *Journal of Jewish Education* 72, no. 3 (2006): 161–181.

Fenstermacher, Gary D. "The Knower and the Known: The Nature of Knowledge in Research on Teaching." *Review of Research in Education* 20 (1994): 3–56.

Fish, Stanley. "A Classical Education: Back to the Future." *The New York Times*, June 7, 2010. http://opinionator.blogs.nytimes.com/2010/06/07/a-classical-education-back-to-the-future.

Fishbane, Michael. *Sacred Attunement: A Jewish Theology*. Chicago: University of Chicago Press, 2008.

Fox, Seymour, Israel Schleffer, and Daniel Marom, eds. *Visions of Jewish Education*. UK: Cambridge University Press, 2003.

Fraenkel, Jonah. *Darkei Haaggada Vehamidrash*. Masada: Yad LeTalmud, 1991. (Hebrew)

— —. *Iyounim Beolamo Haruchani Shel Sippur Haaggadah*. Tel Aviv: Hakibbutz Hameuchad Publishing House, 1981. (Hebrew)

— —. *Sippur Haaggadah: Ahdout Shel Tohen Vetzura*. Tel Aviv: Hakibutz Hameuchad, 2001. (Hebrew)

Frankena, William K. "A Model for Analyzing a Philosophy of Education." In *Readings in the Philosophy of Education: A Study of Curriculum*, edited by Jane R. Martin, 15–22. Boston: Allyn and Bacon, 1970.

Freire, Paulo. *Pedagogy of the Oppressed*. New York: The Seabury Press, 1972.

— —. *The Politics of Education*. South Hadley: Bergin and Garvey, 1985.

Freire, Paulo and Donaldo P. Macedo. "A Dialogue: Culture, Language, and Race." *Harvard Educational Review* 65, no. 3 (1995): 377–402.

Freud, Sigmund. "Some Reflections on Schoolboy Psychology." In *The Standard Edition of the Complete Psychological Works of Sigmund Freud*, vol. 20, edited and translated by James Strachey, 239–244. London: Hogarth, 1914.

Friedman, Milton. *Essays in Positive Economics*. Chicago: University of Chicago Press, 1966.

Fromm, Erich. *Escape from Freedom*. New York: Avon, 1941.

— —. *To Have or To Be?* New York: Continuum, 2008.

Foucault, Michel. *Discipline and Punish: The Birth of the Prison*. New York: Random House, 1975.

Gabelnick, Faith et al., eds. *Communities: Creating Connections Among Students, Faculty, and Disciplines*. San Francisco: Jossey-Bass, 1990.

Gadamer, Hans-Georg. *Reason in an Age of Science*. Cambridge, MA: MIT Press, 1981.

— —. *Truth and Method*. New York: Continuum, 1996.

Gallagher, Shaun. *Hermeneutics and Education*. Albany: State University of New York Press, 1992.

Gardner, Howard. *Frames of Mind: The Theory of Multiple Intelligences*. New York: Basic Books, 1983.

Germer, Christopher K., Ronald D. Siegel, and Paul R. Fulton, eds. *Mindfulness and Psychotherapy*. New York: Guilford Press, 2005.

Giddens, Anthony. *The Consequences of Modernity*. Cambridge: Polity Press, 1990.

— —. *Modernity and Self-Identity: Self and Society in the Late Modern Age*. Cambridge: Polity, 1991.

Gilligan, Carole. *Joining the Resistance*. Cambridge, UK: Polity Press, 2011.

Green, Arthur. *Tormented Master: The Life and Spiritual Quest of Rabbi Nahman of Bratslav*. Woodstock: Jewish Lights Publishing, 1992.

Green, Maxine. *The Dialectic of Freedom*. New York: Teachers College Press, 1988.

— —. *Teacher as Stranger: Educational Philosophy for the Modern Age*. Belmont: Wadsworth Publishing Company, 1973.Greeno, James G. and Melissa S. Gresalfi. "Opportunities to Learn in Practice and Identity." In *Assessment, Equity, and Opportunity to Learn*, edited by Pamela A. Moss, Diana C. Pullin, Edward H. Haertel, James Paul Gee, and Lauren Jones Young, 170–199. New York: Cambridge University Press, 2008.

Gregory, Tom. "School Reform and the No-Man's-Land of High School Size." Unpublished paper presented on October 18, 1997 at the Journal of Curriculum Theorizing Conference, Bloomington, IN. http://eric.ed.gov/?id=ED451981

Habermas, Jurgen. *The Theory of Communicative Action*. Boston: Beacon Press, 1984.

Hacohen, Rabbi Zadok of Lublin. *Resisei Layla*. Bnei Brak: Yehadut Press, 1967. (Hebrew)

— —. *Tzidkat Hatzadik*. Bnei Brak: Brody Katz, 1973. (Hebrew)

Hadot, Pierre. *Exercices Spirituels et Philosophie Antique*. Paris: Albin Michel, 2002. (French)

Handelman, Susan. "'Knowledge has a Face': The Jewish, the Personal, and the Pedagogical." In *Personal Effects: The Social Character of Scholarly Writing*, edited by Deborah Holdstein and David Bleich, 121–144. Utah: Utah State University Press, 2001.

— —. *Make Yourself a Teacher: Rabbinic Tales of Mentors and Disciples*. Seattle and London: University of Washington Press, 2011.

Hargreaves, Andy. "Emotional Geographies of Teaching." *Teachers College Record* 103 (2001): 1056–1080.

Haroutunian-Gordon, Sophie. *Learning to Teach Through Discussion: The Art of Turning the Soul*. New Haven: Yale University Press, 2009.

— —. *Turning the Soul: Teaching through Conversation in the High School*. Chicago: University of Chicago Press, 1991.

Hawkins, David. "I, Thou, and It." In *The Informed Vision: Essays on Learning and Human Nature*, edited by David Hawkins, 48–62. New York: Agathon Press, 2002.

Hayles, Katherine N. *How We Think: Digital Media and Contemporary Technogenesis*. Chicago: Chicago University Press, 2012.

Heidegger, Martin. *Being and Time*. New York: Harper Perennial, 1962.

——. *Discourse on Thinking*. New York: Harper Torchbooks, 1969.

Heilman, Samuel C. *The People of the Book, Drama, Fellowship, and Religion*. Chicago: University of Chicago Press, 1987.

Helmreich, William. *The World of the Yeshiva: An Intimate Portrait of Orthodox Jewry*. New Haven: Yale University Press, 1982.

Heschel, Abraham Joshua. *Insecurity of Freedom: Essays on Human Existence*. New York: Farrar, Strauss and Giroux, 1967.

——. "The Values of Jewish Education." In *Modern Jewish Educational Thought*, edited by David Wienstein and Michael Yizhar, 24–37. Chicago: The College of Jewish Studies, 1964.

Hesse, Herman. *Magister Ludi: The Glass Bead Game*. Translated by Richard Winston and Clara Winston. New York: Picador USA, 1943. http://www.starcenter.com/glassbead.pdf.

Hirsch, Eric Donald. *The Schools We Need and Why We Don't Have Them*. New York: Anchor Books, 1996.

Hirshman, Marc. *The Stabilization of Rabbinic Culture, 100 CE–350 CE — Texts on Education and Their Late Antique Context*. Oxford: Oxford University Press, 2009.

Holtz, Barry W., Gail Z. Dorph, and Ellen B. Goldring. "Educational Leaders as Teacher Educators: The Teacher Educator Institute— A Case from Jewish Education." *Peabody Journal of Education* 72, no. 2 (1997): 147–166.

Holzer, Elie. "Allowing the Text to Do Its Pedagogical Work: Connecting Moral Education and Interpretive Activity." *Journal of Moral Education* 36, no. 4 (2007): 497–514.

——. "Choosing to Put Ourselves 'at Risk' in the Face of Ancient Texts: Ethical Education through the Hermeneutical Encounter." *International Studies in Hermeneutics and Phenomenology* 8, edited by Andre Wiercinski. Berlin: LIT Verlag, 2015, 415–438.

——. "Conceptions of the Study of Jewish Texts in Teachers' Professional Development." *Religious Education* 97, no. 4 (2002): 377–403.

——. *A Double-Edged Sword: Military Activism in the Thought of Religious Zionism*. Bar Ilan University: The Faculty of Law and Shalom Hartman Institute Press, 2008. (Hebrew)

——. "Educational Aspects of Hermeneutical Activity in Text Study." In *Modes of Educational Translation: Studies in Jewish Education*, edited by Jonathan Cohen and Elie Holzer, 205–240. Jerusalem: Magnes Press, 2009.

——. "'Either a Havruta Partner of Death': A Critical View on the Interpersonal Dimensions of Havruta Learning." *The Journal of Jewish Education* 75 (2009): 130–149.

——. "Ethical Dispositions in Text Study." *Journal of Moral Education* 36, no. 1 (2007): 37–49.

——. "'Sfat Emet' Homilies in the Light of Paul Ricoeur's 'Work of the Text.'" *Da'aT, A Journal of Jewish Philosophy and Kabbalah*. (forthcoming). (Hebrew)

——. "Teachers' Learning and the Investigation of Practice." *Mechkarei Morashtenu* 2, no. 3 (2004): 291–302. (Hebrew)

——. "Welcoming Opposition: *Havruta* Learning and Montaigne's *The Art of Discussion*." *The Journal of Moral Education* 44, no. 1 (2015): 64–80.

——. "What Connects 'Good' Teaching, Text Study and Havruta Learning? A Conceptual Argument." *Journal of Jewish Education* 72 (2006): 183–204.

Holzer, Elie and Orit Kent. "Havruta Learning: What Do We Know and What Can We Hope to Learn?" In *International Handbook on Jewish Education*, edited by Helena Miller, Lisa Grant, and Alex Pomson, 407–418. New York: Springer, 2011.

Holzer, Elie with Orit Kent. *A Philosophy of Havruta: Understanding and Teaching the Art of Text Study in Pairs*. Brighton: Academic Studies Press, 2013.

hooks, bell. *Teaching Community: A Pedagogy of Hope*. London: Routledge, 2003.

Horovitz, Isaiah Halevi. *Shnei luchot habrit*. Warsaw: n.p., 1930. (Hebrew)

Hunt, David E. *Beginning with Ourselves: In Practice, Theory and Human Affairs*. Cambridge, MA: Brookline Book, 1987.

Irwin, Terence I. "Plato's Objection to the Sophists." In *The Greek World*, edited by Anton Powell, 568–590. London: Routledge, 1997.

Isaacs, William. *Dialogue and the Art of Thinking Together*. New York: Doubleday, 1999.

Iser, Wolfgang. *Act of Reading: A Theory of Aesthetic Response*. Baltimore: Johns Hopkins University Press, 1978.

——. *The Range of Interpretation*. New York: Columbia University Press, 2000.

Ivie, Stan D. *On the Wings of Metaphor*. San Francisco: Credo Gap Press, 2003.

Jaffee, Martin S. "A Rabbinic Ontology of the Written and Spoken Word: On Discipleship, Transformative Knowledge, and the Living Texts of Oral Torah." *Journal of the American Academy of Religion* 65, no. 3 (1996): 525–549.

——. *Torah in the Mouth: Writing and Oral Tradition in Palestinian Judaism 200 BCE–400 CE*. New York: Oxford University Press, 2001.

James, William. *The Varieties of Religious Experience: A Study in Human Nature, Being the Gifford Lectures on Natural Religion Delivered at Edinburgh in 1901–1902*. London: Longman, Greens and Co., 1902.

Janicaud, Dominique, Jean-François Courtine, Jean-Louis Chrétien, Michel Henry, Jean-Luc Marion, and Paul Ricoeur. *Phenomenology and the 'Theological Turn' — The French Debate*. New York: Fordham University Press, 2000.

Jauss, Hans Robert. *Toward an Aesthetic of Reception*. Minneapolis: University of Minnesota Press, 1982.

Johnson, David W. and Roger T. Johnson. *Cooperation and Competition, Theory and Research*. Edina, MN: Interaction Book Company, 1989.

— —. "Energizing Learning: The Instructional Power of Conflict." *Educational Researcher* 38 (2009): 37–51.

Johnson, David W., Roger T. Johnson, and Karl Smith. "Academic Controversy: Enriching College Instruction through Intellectual Conflict." *ASHE-ERIC Higher Education Report* 25, no. 3 Washington, DC: The George Washington University, 1982.

Jordan, Judith V. "Relational Resilience." In *The Complexity of Connection: Writings from the Stone Center's Jean Baker Miller Training Institute*, edited by Judith V. Jordan, Maureen Walker, and Lisa M. Hartling, 28–46. New York: Guilford Press, 2004.

Katz, Claire E. *Levinas and the Crisis of Humanism*. Bloomington: Indiana University Press, 2013.

Kegan, Robert. *The Evolving Self: Problem and Process in Human Development*. Cambridge, MA: Harvard University Press, 1982.

— —. *In Over Our Heads: The Mental Demands of Modern Life*. Cambridge, MA: Harvard University Press, 1994.

Kerdeman, Deborah. "Some Thoughts about Hermeneutics and Jewish Religious Education." *Religious Education* 93, no. 1 (1998): 29–43.

Kessels, Jos P. A. M. and Fred A. J. Korthagen. "The Relationship between Theory and Practice: Equality or Inequality?" In *Teacher Education for Equality*, edited by Edvard Befring, 357–365. Oslo: Oslo College, 1996.

Korthagen, Fred A. J. and Angelo Vasalos. "From Reflection to Presence and Mindfulness: 30 Years of Developments Concerning the Concept of Reflection in Teacher Education." Paper presented at the EARLI Conference, Amsterdam, August, 2009. http://www.kernreflectie.nl/Media/pdf/EARLI%20paper.pdf

Kosman, Adamiel. *Massekhet Gvarim: Rav Vehakatzav Veod Sippurim*. Jerusalem: Keter, 2002. (Hebrew)

Lakoff, George and Mark Johnsen. *Metaphors We Live By*. London: The University of Chicago Press, 2003.

Lamm, Norman. *Torah Lishmah: In the Works of Rabbi Hayyim of Volozhin and His Contemporaries*. New York: Yeshiva University Press, 1989.

Lasch, Christopher. *The Culture of Narcissism: American Life in an Age of Diminishing Expectations*. New York: Basic Books, 1978.

Leiner, Mordechai Y. *Mei Hashiloach*, vol. 1. Bnei Brak: Mishor Publishing, 2007. (Hebrew)

Levinas, Emmanuel. *Difficult Freedom: Essays on Judaism.* Baltimore: The Johns Hopkins University Press, 1997.

— —. "Judaism and Kenosis." In *In the Time of the Nations,* 112–113. New York: Continuum, 2007.

— —. *Of God Who Comes To Mind.* Stanford: Stanford University Press, 1998.

— —. *Totality and Infinity: An Essay on Exteriority.* Translated by Alphonso Lingis. Dordrecht, The Netherlands: Kluwer Academic Publishers, 1991.

— —. "Zionisms: Assimilation and New Culture." In *The Levinas Reader,* edited by Sean Hand, 267–288. Cambridge, MA: Basil Blackwell, 1989.

Levisohn, Jon A. "Openness and Commitment: Hans-Georg Gadamer and the Teaching of Jewish Texts." *Journal of Jewish Education* 67, no. 1 (2001): 20–35.

Liebes, Yehuda. "Eros Ve'anti Eros al Hayarden." In *Life as a Sanctuary: Studies in Jewish Psychology,* edited by Schachar Arazi, Michal Fachler, and Baruch Kahana, 157–162. Tel Aviv: Yediot Acharonot Publishing, 2004.

Loewenthal, Tali. "Early Hasidic Teachings—Esoteric Mysticism, or a Medium of Communal Leadership?" *Journal of Jewish Studies* 37 (1986): 58–75.

Lyons, Nona, ed. *Handbook of Reflection and Reflective Inquiry: Mapping a Way of Knowing for Professional Reflective Inquiry.* New York: Springer, 2010.

Lyotard, Jean-François. *The Postmodern Condition: A Report on Knowledge.* Manchester: Manchester University Press, 1984.

— —. *The Postmodern Explained to Children: Correspondence, 1982–1985.* London: Turnaround, 1992.

Mack, Chananel. "Shiveim Panim LaTorah: Al Guilgulo shel Mussag." In *Jubilee Book in the Honor of Rabbi Mordechai Breuer: Articles in Jewish Studies,* vol. 2, edited by Moshe Bar-Asher, 449–462. Jerusalem: Akademon Press, 1992. (Hebrew)

Maharal. *Derech Chaim.* Jerusalem: Sifrei Yehadut, 1984. (Hebrew)

— —. *Netivot Olam.* Jerusalem: Sifrei Yehadut, 1984. (Hebrew)

— —. *Sefer Be'er Hagolah.* Jerusalem: Sifrei Yehadut, 1984. (Hebrew)

Maimonides. *Guide for the Perplexed.* New York: Cosimo Classics, 2007.

— —. *The Laws of Torah Study. Mishneh Torah.* Jerusalem: Yerushalem Pub., 1970.

Manguel, Alberto. *The Library at Night.* New Haven: Yale University Press, 2006.

Marcel, Gabriel. *Being and Having.* Translated by Katharine Farrer. Westminster: Dacre Press, 1949.

Mark, Tzvi. *Revelation and Repair in the Explicit and Esoteric Writings of Rabbi Nachman of Bratslav.* Jerusalem: Magnes Press, 2011.

Marom, Daniel. "Educational Implications of Michael Fishbane's *Sacred Attunement: A Jewish Theology.*" *Journal of Jewish Education* 74 (2008): 29–51.

McCombs, Barbara L. *Learner-Centered Classroom Practices and Assessments: Maximizing Student Motivation, Learning & Achievement.* Thousand Oaks: Corwin Press, 2007.

McCourt, Frank. *Teacher Man: A Memoir.* Old Tappan: Scribner, 2006.

Meier, Deborah. *The Power of Their Ideas.* Boston: Beacon, 1995.

— —. "Supposing That . . ." *Phi Delta Kappan* 78, no. 4 (1996): 271–276.

Meijer, Paulien C., Fred A. J. Korthagen, and Angelo Vasalos. "Supporting Presence in Teacher Education: The Connection Between the Personal and Professional Aspects of Teaching." *Teaching & Teacher Education* 25, no. 2 (2009): 297–308.

Mendelsund, Fred. *What We See When We Read.* New York: Vintage Books, 2014.

Merriam-Webster's Collegiate Dictionary. 11th ed. Springfield, MA: Merriam-Webster, 2003. http://www.merriam-webster.com/.

Mezirow, Jack. "Perspective Transformation." *Adult Education Quarterly* 28, no. 2 (1978): 100–110.

— —. "Transformative Learning: Theory to Practice." *New Directions for Adult and Continuing Education* 74 (1997): 5–12.

Mezirow, Jack and Associates. *Learning as Transformation: Critical Perspectives on a Theory in Progress.* San Francisco: Jossey-Bass, 2000.

Michea, Jean-Claude. *L'Enseignement de L'ignorance et ses Conditions Modernes.* Paris: Climats, 1999. (French)

Montaigne, Michel de. *The Complete Works: Essays, Travel Journal, Letters.* Translated by Donald M. Frame. New York, London, and Toronto: Everyman's Library, 2003.

Munby, Hugh. "Metaphor in the Thinking of Teachers: An Exploratory Study." *Journal of Curriculum Studies* 18 (1986): 197–219.

Nachman of Breslov. *Likutey Moharan.* Jerusalem: Breslov Research Institute, 1990.

Noddings, Nel. *Caring: A Feminine Approach to Ethics and Moral Education.* Berkeley: University of California Press, 2003.

— —. *The Challenge to Care in Schools: An Alternative Approach to Education,* 2nd ed. New York: Teachers College Press, 2005.

Nussbaum, Martha C. *The Fragility of Goodness: Luck and Ethics in Greek Tragedy and Philosophy.* Cambridge: Cambridge University Press, 1986.

— —. *Love's Knowledge: Essays on Philosophy and Literature.* New York: Oxford University Press, 1990.

——. *Not for Profit: Why Democracy Needs the Humanities*. Princeton: Princeton University Press, 2010.

Oakshott, Michael. *The Voice of Liberal Learning: Michael Oakeshott on Education*. New Haven: Yale University Press, 1989.

Paley, Vivian G. "On Listening to What Children Say." *Harvard Educational Review* 56, no. 2 (1986): 122–131.

Palmer, Parker J. *The Courage to Teach, Exploring the Inner Landscape of a Teacher's Life*. San Francisco: Jossey-Bass Publishers, 2009.

Paloutzian, Raymond F. "Psychology of Religious Conversion and Spiritual Transformation." In *The Oxford Handbook of Religious Conversion*, edited by Lewis R. Rambo and Charles E. Farhadian, 209–239. Oxford: Oxford Handbooks Online, 2014. http://www.oxfordhandbooks.com.

Patočka, Jan. *Body, Community, Language and World*. Edited by James Dodd. Translated by Erazim Kohák. Chicago: Open Court, 1998.

Picard, Max. *The Human Face*, 1st ed. Translated by Guy Endore. Wichita, KS: Farrar & Rinehart, 1930.

Pinchevski, Amit. *By Way of Interruption: Levinas and the Ethics of Communication*. Pittsburgh: Duquesne University Press, 2005.

Plato. "Gorgias." In *The Dialogues of Plato*, vol. 2, 267–422. Translated by Benjamin Jowett. Oxford: Oxford University Press, 1892. http://classics.mit.edu/Plato/gorgias.html.

——. "Meno." In *The Dialogues of Plato*, vol. 2, 1–64. Translated by Benjamin Jowett. Oxford: Oxford University Press, 1892. http://classics.mit.edu/Plato/menon.html.

——. "Theaetetus." In *The Dialogues of Plato*, vol. 4, 107–200. Translated by Benjamin Jowett. Oxford: Oxford University Press, 1892. http://classics.mit.edu/Plato/theaetetus.html.

Provenzo, Eugene J., Gary N. McCloskey, Robert B. Kottkamp, and Marylin Kohn. "Metaphor and Meaning in the Language of Teachers." *Teacher College Record* 90 (1989): 551–573.

Raider-Roth, Miriam. *Trusting What You Know: The High Stakes of Classroom Relationships*. San Francisco: Josey-Bass, 2005.

Raider-Roth, Miriam and Elie Holzer. "Learning to be Present: How Hevruta Learning Can Activate Teachers' Relationships to Self, Other and Text." *The Journal of Jewish Education* 75, no. 3 (2009): 216–239.

Raider-Roth, Miriam, Vicky Stieha, and Billy Hensley. "Rupture and Repair: Episodes of Resistance and Resilience in Teachers' Learning." *Teaching and Teacher Education* 28 (2012): 493–502.

Ratner, Joseph, ed. *Intelligence in the Modern World — John Dewey's Philosophy*. New York: The Modern Library, 1939.

Ratzerdorfer-Rosen, Gila. "Empathy and Aggression in Torah Study: Analysis of a Talmudic Description of Havruta Learning." In *Wisdom from All My Teachers*, edited by Jeffrey Sacks and Susan A. Handelman, 249–263. Jerusalem and New York: Urim Publications, 2003.

Ravitch, Diane. *Left Back: A Century of Battles Over School Reform*. New York: Simon & Schuster, 2000.

Ravitzky, Aviezer. "HaShalom Kemusag Kosmi, Utopia Vehistoria Bahagut Hayehudit Beyemei Habeinayim." *Da'at—A Journal of Jewish Philosophy and Kabbalah* 17 (1986): 5–22. (Hebrew)

Rawidowicz, Simon. *Iyounim BeMachshevet Israel*, vol. 1. Jerusalem: Rubin Mass, 1969. (Hebrew)

Ricoeur, Paul. *The Conflict of Interpretations*. Evanston: Northwestern University Press, 1974.

— —. *Figuring the Sacred: Religion, Narrative and Imagination*. Minneapolis: Fortress Press, 1995.

— —. *Hermeneutics and the Human Sciences*. Cambridge: Cambridge University Press, 1981.

— —. *Interpretation Theory: Discourse and the Surplus of Meaning*. Fort Worth: Texas Christian University Press, 1976.

— —. "Language is my Kingdom." Translated by Charles E. Reagan. *Esprit* 23 (1955): 192–205.

— —. *The Rule of Metaphor—Multi-Disciplinary Studies of the Creation of Meaning in Language*. Toronto, Buffalo, and London: University of Toronto Press, 1975.

— —. *The Symbolism of Evil*. Boston: Beacon Press, 1967.

Riley-Taylor, Elaine. *Ecology, Spirituality, and Education: Curriculum for Relational Knowing*. New York: Peter Lang, 2002.

Rodgers, Carol and Miriam Raider-Roth. "Presence in Teaching." *Teachers and Teaching: Theory and Practice* 12, no. 3 (2006): 265–287.

Rogers, Carl R. "The Interpersonal Relationship: The Core of Guidance." In *Person to Person: The Problem of Being Human, a New Trend in Psychology*, edited by Carl Rogers, Barry Stevens, Eugene Gendlin, John Shlien, and Wilson Van Dusen, 85–101. Lafayette: Real People Press, 1967.

Rogoff, Barbara. *Apprenticeship in Thinking*. New York: Oxford University Press, 1990.

Rousseau, Jean Jacques. *Emile or Concerning Education*. Boston: Heath and Company, 1889.

Rubenstein, Jeffrey L. *Stories of the Babylonian Talmud*. Baltimore: The Johns Hopkins University Press, 2010.

— —. *Talmudic Stories: Narrative Art, Composition and Culture*. Baltimore: Johns Hopkins University Press, 2003.

Ruzin, Rabbi Yosef. *Tsafnat Pa-aneach*, vol. 4. Jerusalem: Maor, 1962. (Hebrew)

Ryken, Leland. "Formalist and Archetypal Criticism." In *Contemporary Literary Theory: A Christian Appraisal*, edited by Clarence Walhout and

Leland Ryken, 1–23. Grand Rapids, MI: Eerdmans Publishing Co., 1991.

Sagi, Avi. *Ne-emanut Hilchatit: Ben Petichut Lesgirut*. Ramat Gan: Bar Ilan University Press, 2012. (Hebrew)

——. *The Open Canon: On the Meaning of Halachic Discourse*. New York: Continuum, 2007.

——. "The Punishment of Amalek in Jewish Tradition: Coping with the Moral Problem." *The Harvard Theological Review* 87 (1994): 323–346.

Scheer, Steven C. *Dancing with the Daffodils: Essays on Life and Love and Letters*. USA: Bird Brain Publishing, 2011.

Schon, Donald A. *The Reflective Practitioner: How Professionals Think in Action*. USA: Basic Books, 1983.

Schutz, Alfred. *Collected Papers*, vol. 1. Edited by Maurice Natanson. The Hague: Martinus Nijhoff, 1967.

——. *On Phenomenology and Social Relations*. Edited by Helmut R. Wagner. Chicago: University of Chicago Press, 1970.

Schwab, Joseph J. "Eros and Education: A Discussion of One Aspect of Discussion." In *Science, Curriculum, and Liberal Education: Selected Essays*, edited by Ian Westbury and Neil J. Wilkof, 105–132. Chicago and London: The University of Chicago Press, 1978.

Senge, Peter M., C. Otto Scharmer, Joseph Jaworski, and Betty Sue Flowers. *Presence: Exploring Profound Change in People, Organizations, and Society*. London: Nicolas Brealey, 2004.

Shapiro, Harvey Svi. *Losing Heart: The Moral and Spiritual Miseducation of America's Children*. London: Routledge, 2004.

Sharon, Todd. *Learning from the Other: Levinas, Psychoanalysis, and Ethical Possibilities in Education*. Albany: Sunny Press, 2003.

Shor, Ira. *Empowering Education*. Chicago: University of Chicago Press, 1992.

Shuell, Thomas J. "Teaching and Learning as Problem Solving." *Theory into Practice* 29 (1990): 102–108.

Shulman, Lee S. *The Signature Pedagogies of the Professions of Law, Medicine, Engineering, and the Clergy: Potential Lessons for the Education of Teachers*. Paper presented at the National Research Council's Center for Education, February 6–8, 2005. http://www.taylorprograms.org/images/Shulman_Signature_Pedagogies.pdf.

——. "Theory, Practice and the Education of Professionals." *The Elementary School Journal* 98, no. 5 (1998): 511–526.

Shultz, Kathy. *Listening: A Framework for Teaching Across Differences*. New York and London: Teachers College Press, 2003.Simondon, Gilbert. "The Genesis of the Individual." In *Incorporations*, edited by Jonathan Crary and Sanford Kwinter, 297–319. New York: Zone Books, 1992.

——. *L'individu et sa genèse physico-biologique*. Paris: PUF, 1964. (French)

Sizer, Theodore. *Horace's Compromise: The Dilemma of the American High School*. New York: Houghton Mifflin Co, 1984.

Skorczewski, Dawn. *Teaching One Moment at a Time: Disruption and Repair in the Classroom*. Amherst: University of Massachusetts Press, 2005.

Smith, Adam. *An Inquiry into the Nature and the Causes of the Wealth of Nations*. Edited by Kathryn Sutherland. Oxford: Oxford University Press, 1993.

Stampfer, Shaul. *Lithuanian Yeshivas of the Nineteenth Century: Creating a Tradition of Learning*. Oxford: Littman Library of Jewish Civilization, 2012.

Steiner, George. *After Babel: Aspects of Language and Translation*. New York and London: Oxford University Press, 1975.

— —. *Real Presences*. Chicago: University of Chicago Press, 1991.

Stern, David. *Midrash and Theory: Ancient Exegesis and Contemporary Literary Studies*. Evanston: Northwestern University Press, 1996.

Stiegler, Bernard. *La Télécratie contre la Démocracie*. Paris: Champs, 2006. (French)

— —. *Reenchanter le Monde*. Paris: Flammarion 2006. (French)

Stodolsky, Susan, Gail Z. Dorph, and Sharon Feiman-Nemser. "Professional Culture and Professional Development in Jewish Schools: Teachers' Perceptions and Experiences." *Journal of Jewish Education* 72, no. 2 (2006): 91–108.

Theonas, Georgios, Dave Hobbs, and Dimitrios Rigas. "The Effect of Facial Expressions on Students in Virtual Educational Environments." *International Scholarly and Scientific Research & Innovation* 1, no. 11 (2007): 334–341.

Thomas, Clark. "Sharing the Importance of Attentive Listening Skills." *Journal of Management Education* 23 (1999): 216–223.

Tompkins, Jane. "Learning From the Workplace: Professional Life as an Opportunity for Personal Growth." In *Living the Questions: Essays Inspired by the Life and Work of Parker J. Palmer*, edited by Sam M. Intrator, 89–97. San Francisco: Jossey-Bass, 2005.

Tronick, Edward Z. and Kathrine M. Weinberg. "Depressed Mothers and Infants: Failure to Form Dyadic States of Consciousness." In *Postpartum Depression and Child Development*, edited by Lynne Murray and Peter Cooper, 54–84. New York: Guilford Press, 1997.

Urbach, Efraim Elimelech. *Chazal: Emunot Vedeot*. Jerusalem: Magnes Press, 1979. (Hebrew)

Valdes, Mario J., ed. *Phenomenological Hermeneutics and the Study of Literature*. Toronto: University of Toronto Press, 1987.

Van Eemeren, Frans H., Rob Grootendorst, Ralph H. Johnson, Christian Plantin, and Charles A. Willard. *Fundamentals of Argumentation Theory: A Handbook of Historical Backgrounds and Contemporary Developments*. New Jersey: Lawrence Erlbaum Associates, 1996.

Van Manen, Max. *Phenomenology of Practice: Meaning-Giving Methods in Phenomenological Research and Writing.* Walnut Creek: Left Coast Press, 2014.

Vangelisti, Anita L., Mark L. Knapp, and John A. Daly. "Conversational Narcissism." *Communication Monographs* 57 (1990): 251–274.

Vygotsky, Lev S. *Mind in Society: The Development of Higher Psychological Processes.* Cambridge, MA: Harvard University Press, 1978.

Waquet, Francoise. *Les Enfants de Socrate: Filiation Intellectuelle et Transmission du Savoir, XVIIe–XXIe siècle.* Paris: Albin Michel, 2008. (French)

Weinsheimer, Joel. *Philosophical Hermeneutics and Literary Theory.* New Haven: Yale University Press, 1991.

Weiss, Joseph. "Torah Study in Early Hasidism." In *Studies in East European Jewish Mysticism and Hasidism,* edited by David Goldstein, 56–68. Oxford: Littman Library, 1985.

Welton, Michael. "Listening, Conflict and Citizenship: Towards a Pedagogy of Civil Society." *International Journal of Lifelong Education* 21 (2002): 197–208.

Wentzer, T. Schwarz. "Toward a Phenomenology of Questioning: Gadamer on Questions and Questioning." In *Gadamer's Hermeneutics and the Art of Conversation: International Studies in Hermeneutics and Phenomenology,* vol. 2, edited by Andrzej Wiercinski, 243–266. Berlin: Lit Verlag, 2011.

Wexler, Philip. *Becoming Somebody: Toward a Social Psychology of School.* London and Washington DC: Falmer, 1992.

Wiesel, Elie. "Rabbi Johanan and Resh Lakish." In *Alei Shefer: Studies in the Literature of Jewish Thought, Presented to Rabbi Dr. Alexandre Safran,* edited by Moshe Hallamish, 175–194. Ramat-Gan: Bar-Ilan University Press, 1990.

Wilde, Oscar. *The Complete Fairy Tales of Oscar Wilde.* Stilwell, KS: Digireads. com Publishing, 2006.

Zagzebski, Linda T. *Virtues of the Mind: An Inquiry into the Nature of Virtue and the Ethical Foundations of Knowledge.* Cambridge: Cambridge University Press, 1996.

Zeichner, Kenneth M. *Educating Teachers for Cultural Diversity.* Michigan State University: National Center for Research, 1992.

Index

CPSIA information can be obtained
at www.ICGtesting.com
Printed in the USA
JSHW051944220621
16158JS00002B/36